JOURNEYS OF SECOND ADULTHOOD

A Woman's Search for Higher Ground

21st Century Viewpoints on the Human Condition

STORIES ◇ POEMS ◇ ESSAYS

Geraldine Schwartz, Ph.D.

Order this book online at www.trafford.com
or email orders@trafford.com

Most Trafford titles are also available at major online book retailers.

Print information available on the last page.

ISBN: 978-1-4251-0010-0 (sc)

Trafford rev. 08/24/2020

 www.trafford.com

North America & international
toll-free: 844-688-6899 (USA & Canada)
fax: 812 355 4082

In the end, it will not be what we talked about, but what we did, how we acted, where we put our time and energy, because by everything we do we model and mentor what we value. Our lives speak loudly.

Cover photograph taken on top of an extinct volcano, just climbed in the Galapagos Islands.

Dedications

To Desmond, my traveling companion whose love and support makes Journeys of Second Adulthood possible in real life.

To all my children: and especially to my grandchildren Jamie, Chantelle, Justin, Haley, Geoffrey, Ben and Will for whom these essays have been written.

Contents

Foreword

Those who find their way to this book, or perhaps have been found by this book, are indeed privileged. In these pages you will hear in your mind a voice that simply embraces you with its authenticity. I am especially privileged to know the voice and the woman behind it in my personal life; but never have I heard it break through with such clarity and passion as in this collection of reminiscences, poems and essays.

Geraldine Schwartz, Gerri to her friends, is a great spirit. I know that it is with some trepidation that she shares the intimate details of her personal struggle in the pages of the following Prologue. But what woman, I wonder, could not be moved by this story of emergence from despair, and almost certainly strengthened if she, too, is on a similar path? And what man or woman could not be captivated by the lyrical exuberance and insightful wisdom of the poems? I encourage you to begin there so that you meet in her full authentic self the woman who will then lead you through the reflections in her essays of Second Adulthood.

Gerri and I have been on the journey she describes together, but her voice is fully her own. I encourage you, if you can, to read the text from beginning to end, and in one sitting, if that is possible. If you do, you will find yourself swept along by the passionate reasoning, by the easy handling of complex scientific concepts, but above all by the wise, consistent optimism about the potential of people to rise to meet the challenges that face us. I would then encourage you to re-read each essay thoughtfully to mine and embrace as your own the wisdom it contains.

In these essays, written over an eleven year period from 1993 to 2004, you will hear Gerri proclaim that the basic principle of life is to engage in win-win relationships, that the threats of terrorism and violence contain the seeds of hope, and that the content of human consciousness is overwhelmingly disposed toward the good, which will lead us to a safe and decent future.

For me, Gerri's essay on Leadership is one of the most compelling statements in the book, describing as it does a transcendence from the so-called heroes of past conquest to the new heroes of "right action." But then who could not be moved by her impassioned denunciation of anti-Semitism and not respond to her call to action to overcome such evil with fierce moral courage and to "raise ten million flags for good?" And who could not be touched by her description of the new sensitivity she sees unfolding in the minds of men and women everywhere, which is but the tiny microcosm of the "real macrocosm" that is moving to emerge?

If you allow yourself to flow, this book will take you on a truly engaging and uplifting journey. I encourage you to set out with Gerri as your guide and at the end find yourself empowered to not only change your own future, but also the future of "all those exposed to your shining model."

Good traveling to all of you!

Desmond Berghofer
April 2006

Prologue

First Adulthood

It was my fortieth birthday. I was filled with the pervasive sadness that comes from being unrecognized at times of special occasion. The kitchen was filled with the scent of twelve red roses sent by a friend and recent house guest. The irony of such an intimate and loving gift sent by a relative stranger did not escape me. My husband of twenty years was preoccupied with his own private demons. The kids were expecting the dinner I was cooking.

Endings don't always come in spectacular ways. This was the beginning of the end of my first adulthood.

It had been twenty years since I stepped forward into the adult world. My life was good and full of accomplishment, marriage, financial security, children and three more university degrees along with the professional success and busy life required to support all of the above.

My psyche took two separate roads. By day the journey was full of colour and intensity fuelled by my natural exuberance. Joy that followed from the success of a client, a special invitation to a conference, praise for any job well done, warmth and returned friendship took quiet pride of place to be savoured alone. Reporting of success was threatening and unwelcome at home. Gradually the power of my daytime self grew to the place where living without joy or hope for joy was no longer possible. The two selves struggled... and one finally crashed bringing both down together.

Dreams of Decision

On the rug
In front of the fire
Two spirits
Wrestle for my soul.

One... old, wise and proud,
Eyes clear and strong,
She reminds me of
My past sorrows,
My youthful mistakes,
My moments of acute pain
And deep distress.

I recognize myself in her.

The other... young, fresh, eager,
Eyes brimming with joy and hope,
She points to the diplomas
Of my successes.

I recognize myself in her.

I am transfixed
Watching this fight.
I long to tip the scales
In favour of hope,
But I cannot.
The stronger of the two
will win,
And I
Can only watch.

I have been writing poetry since childhood... as far back as I can remember poems emerged always whole to reflect a moment of intense clarity of thought. They were usually private, hidden away in the folders that contained the nooks and crannies of my life. I decided to use a pen name to protect my identity as a professional even further in case anyone found the evidence. I chose a short version of the name of my favourite grandmother, Lea Star.

As I moved full speed towards second adulthood, new fearlessness about sharing honest feelings eased the journey. Some examples of the colour and measure of the emotional turmoil and extra sensitivity to what was really going on are included here to tell the personal story of one woman's journey, in the hope that they may touch the heart and so illuminate the journey of others.

I left my marriage and the security of my first adulthood with great sadness, overwhelming guilt, and a choking feeling of great failure. Tears were continually near the surface held at bay by the daytime need to survive and serve a new and fragile practice. After work I entered the unfamiliar territory of deeply grey moods. I needed to heal both body and spirit.

In this interim and transition time a few very special friends penetrated the gloom.

Strange Truths

In a state of vulnerability
Nothing – nothing
Reaches as deep
Or touches the heart
More than friendship
Freely given
As if it makes
No difference at all.

Such friendship
Humbles the heart

And makes
Those who wander
Along the same
Secret road
Wonder... how it is
They have come to be
Among their betters.

Yesterday
As you turned
To wave at me
The truth flashed
- that life
Has no better gift
To give.

I began to pay personal attention to people outside the family unit and to appreciate the quality of person and character.

Ode to a Man

*The group
assembles,
Time flow
suspends,
White energy
centers
As the lighted
stage
revolves to where
he sits.*

*Quiet reasoned
words
Set the tone to
Reflect sharp
thought.*

*What pleasure
comes
To a knowing
heart
To feel... such
Quality of mind.*

Time passed ... I walked on the beach a lot... went to fitness class...
spent Saturdays with my daughter. Hard work and travel restored
health and vigor and new friendships grew in barren places. My
daughter turned 18.

I Remember

small child eyes
deep, deep blue
and trusting
walking beside me
two fingers clutched
tightly in hand

embracing
the scholar
good report in hand
and the tired
camper, happy
with good playing

watching
the ballerina and
the basketball player
intense with grace

and the
growing
beautiful
awkward
adolescent
often now
through silent
tears in both pairs
of blue eyes
looking through
the veil of separateness

and the adult
in full, bold
bloom of youth
clear eyed
intelligent
inner beauty
matching the
surface glow.

what Joy in Motherhood!
what profound hope
for a life full
of the awe
wonder and richness
of my own
and more... much
much more.

what love
too
too
much
to say.

Written on my daughter's 18th birthday

And my son began his journey of adulthood

I Remember

baby feet
daring to
walk
run
swim
ski
before their time
fierce in manhood
at three
daring the Devil
to object
to hot dogging
straight down
the steepest hill

watching (heart in mouth)
the ski jump
the high dive
player of hockey
and T ball
feisty with the challenge
to compete and win

and the adolescent
extreme
in mood
and action
down
deeply sad
full of inertia
for study
for routine
resisting discipline
with every fibre

and eager
to water ski
among ocean liners
to cycle into
the unknown
wilderness
and camp.
solid capable
of fixing anything
trustworthy
and very, very smart

adult before his time
striking out
shouldering responsibility
wanting the
prizes of life
with a deeply
rooted need
to strive
to be his
own man.

what Joy in Motherhood!
what profound hope
for a life full
of the awe
wonder and richness
of my own
and more... much
much more.

what love
too
too
much
to say.

Written on my daughter's 18th birthday, when my son was 22.

Almost strangely, breakthroughs of colour re-emerged as I began to reconnect with the self of my youth and childhood. Periods of joy pierced through the gloom again, at first only occasionally and eventually more and more often. As new friendships and opportunity to work towards life goals emerged, one day walking the familiar beach, waves of colour broke through, filling even the darkest part of the canvas with the crackling colour of life... my life... and I drank with the prodigious thirst of a desert dweller.

Energy Exchange

Today
I exchange energy
with the Universe.
Sunlight crackles
through the crisp air.
Snow peaked mountains
stand piercing
the blue blue sky.

My footsteps on the
wet sand exude heat
as the sea laps against
the beach in little
fringes of white surf.
Twelve squat steamers
wait empty on the near horizon,
Ready to swoop up cargo
for wide world markets.
And the western coloured city
of cream and pink and grey
shimmers in the spring air
full of promise.
And
I take the energy of all this
From the majesty of the mountains
and the mist of the melting sea and sky,

From the prosperous commerce of ships at sea,
From the pulsing shimmering city,
From the quack and caw
of the flying birds,
From the child and his mother
playing in the sand.
All flows freely into me
Giving generously of their power
Asking only the same in return.
And
I power up,
Fuel up,
Fill up,
with the rainbow stuff of life
and turn to the tasks at hand
and the journey ahead,
Renewed
Refreshed
Brimming with
Strength
Vitality and
Courage,
To go forth
Pouring out
high octane energy
before me
For further exchange
with my fellow citizens
of the universe.

Written following a walk on Kitsilano Beach, Vancouver, Canada

I searched for fun again

American Fantasy

Excitement fills
The sunlit air
The train stops
Passengers flow out.

Airwaves tinkle with
Child familiar melodies
Conjuring up
Early feelings of delight
And suspending
The traveler's
Bond with reality.

Through the looking glass
A kaleidoscope of colour
Meets the eye.
Fantasy takes
Form and shape
And floods the lightscape
With memories of
Youthful carefree moments.

High energy defies
Time and age
As the journey
Begins in earnest.

Time flows
Sparking...
Electric...
Pulsing with
Hot feelings
Of joy
Sensual
Erotic
Gentle.

The cinebus, careless of
Corner and roadway
Of sixties cities
Sprouts wings
To fly through
Sky and space
Enveloping the senses with
The sweep and majesty of
Snow peaked mountain
And windswept desert
Of ageless America.

Childish tunes
Yankee Doodle
Pop Goes the Weasel
Mingle with the
Grand patriotism of
America the Beautiful
Providing double exposure
For eye and ear
The Grand Old Duke of York
Ten thousand toy men
Marching up to the
Top of the hill
And...
The soldiers of West Point
Smartly uniformed
Stepping in perfect unison
Up counterpane hill.

The soft sweet air
Of California night
Descends and fills
With motion of
Splashing water
Sounds of pirate fights
Ghouls and ghosts
Of a swashbuckling age
Cannons fire
Houses and souls burn
While we paddle

Continued next page

In awe through
This bloody history
In the lighthearted
Rhythm of dreams .

To stand in crowds
At roadsides
Waiting the big parade
The March of the
Childhood in us begins
The Queen of Hearts
And Alice
Winnie the Pooh
Mickey... Donald
Snow White
Walking trees
Ugly dwarfs
Tweedle Dum and Dee
And fairy godmothers.
In motion of
Pondering bears
And elephants
Skipping fairies
Or silly frenzy
Of mad hatter.

This glittering carousel
Of light and sound
Tunes trembling senses
To highest pitch and
Invades deepest
Memory spaces
With waves of
Gaudy colour
To impress the
Moment on the
Inner slate
Of self.

Written after a trip to Disneyland

And finally I began to consider real relationships with potential partners, based on who I had truly become, a mature woman, strong and confident enough to look for equals in friendship. I would mother, nurture and care for, only children, my children and those who crossed my path professionally. I craved, valued and looked for adult relationships with strong men and women, but especially men. They crossed my path and paid attention... and so did I... they had unique and special gifts to give .. time passed... I collected these special friendships like a string of exquisite pearls... a short interval of time was enough... we met in my city, but especially in exotic places all over the world where I worked and traveled for adventure .. I thought this would be enough... I guarded my deepest heart space, fiercely willing now to walk alone.

And yet if only I could find the kind of love that I read about in the poetry of Pablo Neruda or the novels of fantasy and romance... just in case, I would make my statement on the impossible and expect nothing.

On Loving

Strong men who spend a lifetime
Looking to the needs of others
Are amazed to find
The ways of loving of strong women
Is different from love
Received in gratitude or
In response to their caregiving.

It caters to a deep unspoken
Need in them that looks to
Nourishing the very strength
On which their soul is built.

It meets them freely in full stride
To move alongside in the synchrony
Of their natural rhythm
With the unbounded joy of being alive.

Such loving provides the ultimate challenge
To grow beyond known strength,
To risk new and powerful states of being
They never dared hope existed.

Energy from such loving
Could transform the very planet,
And it will!

At this point in the journey the men who crossed my path were tumbling out of marriages of long standing and newly alone, beginning unfamiliar journeys. Almost always they were caring for first wives and families who, now estranged from them, saw them as 'meal tickets' for themselves and their vulnerable children. Many suffered from the emotional blackmail they felt they deserved. Guilt-ridden, they put aside their own emotional needs and soldiered on. Some very few could handle all that and rebuild their own emotional lives. I recognized them as fellow travelers.

I was ready again to live fully... if only... but even the thought of readiness filled me with fear... six years had passed... I had rebuilt a good life... full of colour, good work, travel... friendships.

and then I met a friend... maybe more than a friend
and he met me...
Courage was needed...
I began to sing courage songs.

Of My Life

And the rest...
I will make
no less than wonderful...

Be gone you timid heart!
Wonderful
Needs
Another kind
Of strength.

Let the trumpet play courage songs
That I may march
Head high.

Let each muscle in
Newly grown wings
Pull its weight.

That I may gather
Every ounce of fuel
For lift off.

Boost me free strong heart
To fly over
Majestic mountains
At dizzy height
For an eagle eye view
Of even higher
Peaks beyond.

Yes
Yes
Be gone you timid heart!

The journey from alone to together was full of potential and danger... but the Journey of Second Adulthood was just at the horizon. Somehow as I inched forward... and retreated... and moved forward again... a new life, full of colour, full of the deep texture and the intensity of love, romance, adult friendship and even collegial work produced a deep longing for the impossible... I hesitated afraid to be hurt... and if I was left to my own devices too long the opportunity would have passed with the ultimate life lasting regret of what could have been.

But I was not alone... encouraged, invited, embraced and finally asked I dared...

We married on August 3, 1989.

Challenges abounded... his young family needed sustenance and nurture... a move of cities, professional status and the blending of two fully grown persona different in every possible way, by country of birth, by religion, by temperament needed to take place... work and play and love all needed balance in both separate and joined spaces. This is a very different task from the first joining of two youthful spirits without experience or baggage.

And yet for two adults in a relationship of love, respect and friendship this part of the journey works, and the Journey of Second Adulthood begins with Yes to life.

Yes (1)

Yes is an affirmation
*   built on a thousand noes.*

No to
* death, pain,*
* sickness,*
* sadness,*
* and bad compromise.*

No to
* lethargy,*
* fuzzy thinking,*
* mediocrity,*
* and boredom.*

Yes begins
* with intention*
* to take little yes steps.*

Yes to
* vigour*
* to strength,*
* and striving,*
* to hard work*
* and homework,*
* to study*
* and learning,*
* and thinking,*
* to writing,*
* and being.*

Yes to
* embarking on journeys,*
* to questing and questions.*

Yes to
* dancing*
* and singing,*
* to poetry,*
* music,*
* and laughter.*

Yes to
* feeling*
* and friendship,*
* to well-being,*
* to good food,*
* and good drinking,*
* to beach walks,*
* to popcorn and movies,*
* to fireside chats*
* and pillow talking.*

Yes to
* fun places,*
* to wilderness spaces,*
* to mountains and climbing,*
* to playing and dreaming,*
* to planning and deep seeing.*

And when the chorus of yeses
* rings out in celebration,*
* fueling the heart with wild courage,*

It's easy
* to take giant leaps*
* to say:*
* YES*
* to growing,*
* to being,*
* to soaring,*
* to living,*
* to loving.*

To me
* to you,*
* to us.*

So
* I can,*
* I will,*
* And I do!*

We began to work with champions and leaders. Together we put on events with world class partners from both our former lives. Our work with leaders facing the massive demands of a changing and increasingly global village took us across the country and to foreign places.

We traveled in and into each other's youthful and childhood places, to Australia and to Montreal, to bridge the quarter century we had missed in each other's lives.

He, returning to a youthful passion for writing, wrote a magnificent first novel, *The Visioneers, A Courage Story about Belief in the Future*. We put on events to launch the book and ideas into the world, incorporating it in all our professional work, and we launched the international newsletter, "The Visioneer," to provide expression for our growing thinking about the work we were doing. This newsletter is the source of most of the essays in this book.

Our work with champions and leaders brought extraordinary people into our path. We recognized them and as the years flowed by, worked on partnered tasks, each time getting ready for the next one that followed.

Call for the Champions

Pulsing with Herculean energy,
imbued with visions of the impossible,
the Champion,
mind primed by
the God-strength within,
guided by a brilliance
sensed only by cell and nerve,
strains against
the stormy negative turbulence
of our mythic times,
to breakthrough
with bursting heart
to the heaven swept
field and plain
promised
only in our genes.

Knowing the very spirit
of our race
is at stake
let those
who hear this call
of the Shofar*
gather.

The New Year is at hand.

*Shofar: ram's horn used since ancient times to
signal the celebration of the Jewish New Year.

A full life began to emerge as we moved to the next parts of the journey...

Real Riches

Each life flows
toward an unknown source,
carrying the silt swept up
as it passes the rocky
uneven terrain of
river's bottom.

It sweeps along
on currents fast and turbulent
in winter's icy grip,
or through calm
still green pools
languishing in summer's heat.

Most swimmers skim the surface
gathering such a very little.
Others fight the rapids,
or stay to pan for gold.
Only a few explore the depths
where true treasures lie.

They are the ones
who hear well
the cry of
a newborn child,
and feel its mother's
primordial response
gathered in the father's
protective shelter of love.

They are the ones
who reach into the deep
for love of man and woman
too sacred for speaking.

Or see the glory
in all the little things
betwixt life and passage,
from celebration and ceremony,
to mundane meals and sleep,
and both,
mixed with
the ordinary rhythm
of a day's breath.

They muddy
their eager hands
in art and science,
in myth creation
and storytelling,
in idea and business building
thus writing
the very music
of our humanity.

So the river comes
to broader shores
to great bays
open to the source.

Here the swimmers
gather strength
to enter the timeless ocean
graced only with the wealth
the spirit carries.

Sometimes in a split instant
of altered mind and breath
the whole blue green river
comes into view all at once
where, witnessing, stunned
and in awe
these few see
the whole truth appear.

If perchance we break
through such skin of dream
while breath runs through us,
we must urgently this story tell
that others may come
to this rare and hidden shore,
until there are enough
that such a cohort
reborn together
may one day save the earth.

Post scriptum: Maybe such a day
                            is dawning.

A more mature statement of the meaning of Yes emerges.

Yes (2)

Is a way to live
passionately on purpose.

It begins with the
courage to say No
to lethargy
to inertia
to fear.

It stands against
lies
treachery
hatred
and violence.

It begins in the quiet stillness
of a mind at rest.

Yes becomes the canvas
on which life's future
possibilities can be painted.

Yes is honed in the capacity
for awe and wonder.
Yes begins to answer the question,
"What if...?"

In maturity, when life's experiences
have created the container for wiser choices,
Yes is the most profound of choices.

It is built on choices of the past
that cannot be changed.
It is wrought from journeys' ends
and relationships completed.

Yes is built on yesterday's dreams
and tomorrow's most fervent hopes.
Yes is the life force
that heals all wounds
and allows us to emerge whole and in health
at the dawn of a new and better day.

So at this moment
deeply engaged in life
with purpose and intent
I gather my new Yeses
in a divine and sacred list.

Yes to purpose and intention.

Yes to vigour, to excitement and spontaneity.
Yes to colour, to laughter, to joy and to wonder.

Yes to touching roots, to reaching for dreams.
Yes to legacies, treasures and blessings.
Yes to travel, adventure and discovery.
Yes to questing and questions.
Yes to journeys of the heart.
Yes to sacred spaces and wilderness places.

Yes to passion and compassion,
to tenderness, to soft kisses and warm hugs.
Yes to partnership and friendship.
Yes to the ordinary mornings and to sharing
the simple sweet pleasures of love.

Yes to being... to growing...
to giving and getting.
Yes to life...
Le chaim!
To life!

And finally we begin a new part of the journey together. He publishes *Antale: An Allegory of a World Reborn*. I publish these essays and poems as *Journeys of Second Adulthood*, and we start a new leg of this wondrous journey based on what has gone before, the legacy part.

And so we are ready.

Now

Now, looking inward
over a lifetime's
hardwon achievements,
let us celebrate
our time of grace,
and gathering a power
earned of long experience,
let us dare
to think new thoughts,
to love profoundly,
to work hard,
to believe fiercely,
to nurture
with great compassion,
and to vision a future
more wondrous than anything past,
for ourselves
and for the children of
this world and time.

Now, that the power of mind and heart
burst with Amazon spirit
to do,
to be,
to create,
to invent
new solutions for a troubled planet,

let us embark
with adventurous heart
on a journey
so new,
so wisdom based,
so soul focused
that even the gods
and the angels would applaud.

Who will embark with me
on this voyage
of the new champions?
Who will write our story?
Who will record the glory
reflected in our faces
and heard in our voices?

Now we are old enough,
Now we are wise enough
to begin.

Carpe momentum!

Let us seize the moment!

Images
on the
Journey:

▲ At home.

▲ On the speakers circuit.

At work. ▶

On the
Road.

◄ On the Galapagos Islands
overlooking the Pacific
Ocean from the top of an
extinct volcano.

In front of the Parthenon
▶
Athens, Greece.

Introduction

Like a poem, an essay is a self contained vessel for clear, straightforward communication of a thought, or a point of view in a moment in time. The Essays that follow are the accumulation of thoughts building up over time. Written approximately three months apart, they are the results of what was happening in the world at large and in my own life and journeys. They required time and space. You see the beginning paragraphs reflecting the time they were written, always on a holiday, Spring Break, summer, Mother's Day, New Year's, etc. Like the poetry, they are written as a piece flowing out as it were whole from some deep place. For this reason even when they contain substantive information, as many of them do, they are written with all the references at hand, the opinions are uncensored and the beliefs heartfelt and fully my own. The audience for whom they were written were widespread friends, colleagues, or at least acquaintances. For this reason they are in some ways like a conversation with a friend. I assumed they would be read in that vein and over the years have had reasoned and thoughtful feedback that suggested that they put words to the thinking others had been doing in a less focused way.

They are therefore meant to be read as a whole with opportunity to think deeply about the meaning, as if you could have a personal dialogue with the writer.

They reflect thoughtful and illumined moments on my personal journey as a woman, wife, mother, grandmother, professional psychologist, speaker, teacher and leader. It is my special hope that the words and ideas will inspire you to act in positive ways in your own life and on behalf of civil society and the planet that supports us.

As a whole, these essays reflect a personal vision that we will, as a whole species, move forward to that higher ground where we can relate to each other in a respectful compassionate way, and that as mature adults we can live together in ways that bring out the best in each other and in so doing create a multitude of expressions of civil societies across the globe that will serve as a proud legacy to the generations in which our grandchildren grow and become grandparents themselves.

Core Beliefs

It behooves us to look at the stars and ourselves in wonder at our nobility, and to take the energy of that wonder as inspiration to do the work needed to turn the major cultural ethos of our time from cynicism and materialism to a tide of action for transformation and progress towards goodness. So enabled and advantaged we can enter the third millennium with confidence that the future we create will be life-giving and rewarding for those who follow us.

What is important is not what we have done so far, but what we will accomplish in the years ahead. In our youth, full of hope, optimism, determination and enthusiasm, we planned and worked and created ourselves so far. However many chronological years we have lived, we are all at a new beginning. We have a job to do. So let's begin.

We, the citizens, the generations now in charge of the world, and especially those in the developed world, have a sacred trust, inherited from our ancestors, whose generations often sacrificed a good life in their own time for our reward in our time – we have a sacred trust to provide an equal legacy to the generations who follow us.

We Are One in Spirit:

An Action Plan to Manifest Spirit into Deeds of Good Work

A million years ago our hominid ancestors wandered through the savannahs of Africa, part of a web of life with billions of years of evolution behind them. Like our modern primate cousins, our ancient ancestors lived in small family groupings held together by the two core emotional responses of all living creatures: fear and attraction. Fear of enemies and potential environmental catastrophe, and attraction, nurturing and protection of one's own, are core values deeply embedded in our genetic structure. They are as unconscious and key to survival as breathing and eating.

From this biological reality the culture of our species, which arose some 35,000 years ago and spread around the world, was built. Although the languages and the symbols of the groups were different, their purpose and need to survive in the world were built solidly around these two bio-emotional truths. However, if that's all there was to it, we would be expressing our humanity with only a slim layer of consciousness built over a vast unconscious depth, which was unknown and unexamined.

The Richness of Culture and Tradition

Enriching the quality of human experience, ancient religious and philosophical inquiry into the reasons of our existence has developed the culture, the song and the myth whose metaphors and imagery straddle both conscious and unconscious mind.

Over the thousands of generations of our history since the invention of culture, we have taken advantage of the aspects of our brain that make us different from other creatures—a cerebral cortex that can speak, write, plan, imagine, see the future, organize and analyze. This has resulted in an ongoing development of our logical, conscious mind across the planet. In our time this development has led to exponential growth in complexity in every aspect of life. With this human endowment we organize modern life, perform the advances of science and technology, educate our children to higher learning, run integrated economies, and operate huge institutions.

However, despite this progress, the evidence from the 20ᵗʰ century, the most brutal to humanity in known history, has shown that we are still governed by our two bio-emotional needs: fear and attraction. To protect ourselves against our enemies, we have built great fortresses and weapons of mass destruction. To modify our environment and to protect against natural catastrophe, we have used our science and technology—from engineering to medicine, from terrestrial exploration to space travel. At the same time, we have looked after our own, and built our national cultures and economies around attraction.

But even that is not the whole story. Over thousands of years great sages and prophets in every tradition have probed their own very powerful cerebral cortex and have found routes via prayer and meditation to access the power of mind beyond logic. They have left us a rich legacy embedded in various cultural forms that also point to the common heritage of our humanity.

Because we are one species born of a common ancestor, we have come through a thousand language and cultural paths to a common bio-emotional reality: *we are one*, especially at the level of spirit.

To the degree that we intelligently recognize that there are forces outside ourselves, which we may not logically see or understand, we have attributed those forces to a power we call God, Great Spirit, Allah, and so on. Moreover, at a deep fundamental level, we know that this power is one power, just as certainly as we are one species. Indeed, the phenomenon passes the demand test of science for consistency and replication, in that every human culture has some form of spiritual explanation for the phenomenon of existence.

The Gulf between Logic and Spirit

The foregoing discussion points to an important current reality. Over the generations of human history, two separate ways of attaching meaning to life have co-existed in human communities: the conscious logical strand that looks to our secular survival; and the unconscious spiritual strand, which we all recognize to the extent that we access our own spiritual centre. Deeply embedded cultural norms have grown up around each of the two ways of knowing, to the point that the two tend not to intersect.

However, our logical mind fools us, because its proof lies mainly in the senses, often shutting off the larger vision and the wisdom of the right hemisphere of the brain, which is the centre of our imagination and emotional selves.

So it was in 1491 that the logical mind told our forebears of the day that if they sailed far enough out into the ocean's expanse, they would reach the edge and fall off. Fear-based logic told them not to go there—that is, until other people using a deeper and wider imaginative thought process went beyond the current view of logic and discovered the new world.

As science has unwound its amazing understanding and discovery of what we and our planet are made of, down to the smallest quark, the logic of our senses has retreated, and we give credence to the proof from mathematics and intuition, both demanding greater use of the right hemisphere. Here, in the frontal lobes, imaginative thinking sits metaphorically beside the unconscious mind, which knows about the great spiritual force that expresses the truth of our oneness in genetic and molecular terms.

Discovering Common Ground

So we come in our own time to the place where the great religious traditions and the greatest of all conscious, logical-based science are coming to common ground, around the underlying truth of our oneness. However, those who understand this are still very few in number, because to access this wisdom we must go deep within our own minds to touch the essence of our god spirit.

The world is now awash with contradictions among those who limit their understanding to what their logical conscious mind provides, and those who are prepared to go deep into human wisdom to see the larger truths.

To the conscious mind we look different from one another. Our skin, hair, body shape, language and customs make it appear to our senses that we are distinct. Our culture and institutions reinforce this view at every level. They are expressed in our communities as customs of separation and exclusion, manifesting in policies and practice often too subtle for us to notice.

Yet, planetwide the knowledge and wisdom of our spirit prevails. We know we humans are the same, so we send food and peacekeepers to places of war and disaster. We pluck refugees off trees and rooftops in far away lands.

In my opinion, one of the reasons this is happening so massively now is that the television images we see of people in distress, especially women, children and old people, gets right through the logic (that is, those people are too far away and have nothing to do with us) to our image reading and emotional responses centred in our right hemisphere. One image supercedes a thousand left-brain centred logical words, flooding across the corpus collosum and energizing the logical centers to act, to do, and to know that we are one family.

I am amazed at the speed with which this phenomenon is happening in our time. I think it is due to the tremendous power of image and symbol via all our electronic communication systems to show this truth to ordinary people in a powerful way.

As an example, a coloured photo appeared in the *Vancouver Sun* on March 24, 2000 captioned "A Meeting of Faiths." It shows Pope John Paul II sitting between Sheik Taysir Tamimi, a member of the Islamic Higher Committee, and Israel's Chief Rabbi, Israel Meir Lau, in Jerusalem. These men, symbols of their own faith to billions of adherents, sit together in common cause. The words of the Pope, call for a new relationship between the faiths, in which he as Pope regards the Jews as "the elder brothers of the Christians, since both had sprung from the tradition of Abraham and Moses," as of course had the Moslems also.

These are deep and great symbols of common spirit that go *deeply* to the core, bio-emotional levels of the brain and say, "This

5

is our family."

But it is not only religious leaders who are creating such symbolic and powerful new global manifestos. In science and other action the same deeds are afoot, from Doctors Without Borders, recent winners of the Nobel Prize for Peace, to international non-profit agencies, to scientific conferences, to joint international projects in every field of science and medicine, to transnational business endeavours, to art, to music—and the list is too long for these pages. Thus the breakthrough in our time is that deeds follow these symbols in greater and greater numbers. We can best accelerate this process by following suit in big and small ways.

It is important to understand in your own mind and heart and spirit that while there are billions of people who do not access their own consciousness at levels which would allow them to see the bigger picture themselves, in each of them the possibility is present. There are now hundreds of millions who do see, and this cohort gets bigger continuously. Since those who do see are really expressing a truth about our humanity, now solidly grounded in our scientific understanding, the direction in which we are headed is unstoppable. Hence lies the great hope for the future.

What Then Can We Do to Act?

First, reach deep inside yourself to know who your true family is. Know that, since life on our planet began evolving over three billion years ago, no living creature has achieved such high and noble stature and ability, and in that space of great knowing see your elder brother and younger sister in spirit also living on this planet with you at this time.

From this wise and tender place, using your energy, strength and particular talent, move to collaborate with others to create the symbols, the metaphors and deeds that manifest this vision. In so doing you will be practicing and honouring the Laws of Life and Love. Your own spirit will be flooded with a great gladness whose health-giving power will infuse every cell of your body with the energy and passion of our human legacy.

Begin the practice at home. Teach the young this important knowledge. Seek to engage the elders to share their wisdom. Speak out with this wisdom when you see others ignore its truth, not by forcing them to see your way, but by encouraging them to look inside themselves, knowing surely they will meet their humanity, their god and yours within.

April, 2000

Rebuilding the
Global Commons:
Earth Citizens Alert

And so we have come to it—the new millennium and the calendar changing a full four numbers for the first time in 1000 years. What an opportunity we have to build something new, something deeply and profoundly needed, a place for the benefit and nurture of all the species, a real place in the mind and consciousness of all of us alive today, a place that will last, a legacy for our descendants. We are its architects and its pioneers, because we will both bring it into being and become its first citizens. We are building the Global Commons.

In ancient times human groups created common spaces in pastures, at river banks, in town centres, where they could gather, or which they could use in common. This space could not be owned by anyone because it belonged to everyone. Since that time much history has created exclusive private or public ownership restricted to use of an inner group. From this has come nations, boundaries and turf wars of every kind. It has been a long time in human terms since the idea of the Commons existed. However, in our time modern science and technology have shown us the ultimate futility of the protection of some kinds of property for exclusive use.

The air we breathe transcends national boundaries. The water and the earth on our planet are affected by how we care for or neglect any part. Moreover, it is through the air, the water and the earth that the waves of modern communication travel: the radio waves, the video waves, the microwaves and all the waves yet undescribed and unharnessed, that allow us to talk to each other and to see the intimacies of each other's lives for good or for evil purpose.

Thus we see the misery etched on the faces of refugees in Kosovo, East Timor and Chechnya, as if they were in our living room, and the echoes and after images of what we have seen and heard remain in our consciousness.

And we have seen the images of human nobility and striving—the Olympics, the great musical performances, the great dramas of our time—with the same intimacies.

These images transcend every language and boundary, so that wherever people can read, listen to radio, watch television or film, there are those who listen, hear and are ready to connect and act. Thus we are building for the first time in human history a *commons of consciousness of the mind* that no government or villain can control for their own exclusive use. In our time we are moving at great speed to build the technologies and the communication systems that will sustain the Commons.

So far, however, there are few rules and few moral prerogatives that govern behaviour in the commons, just as there were few in the new lands that were discovered in the last 500 years. However, in each nation these rules governed by the cultures of the inner groups have evolved. For the first time in known history we have the opportunities to create the laws and principles by which we may live in common benefit.

New Symbols, Values and Heroes

Some new greatly symbolic institutions are emerging. One of these is the court at The Hague. Justice is the most fundamental of concepts by which we live together. Without it there is no civil society. At last, the world societies, acting as the international community, are taking on the great villains of our times. However, it is important to note that such crimes against humanity were until very recently considered heroic. Have we not given titles of greatness to conquerors of the past from Alexander and Caesar to Napoleon and others, even in this century, who practiced genocide.

Indeed, whether they were considered hero or villain was more determined by their winning or losing than by their deeds. For example, a new book by John Lukacs (*Five Days in London*, Yale University Press, 1999) describes Hitler as the greatest revolutionary of the 20th century—greater than Lenin or Stalin. This same book notes that Hitler's path was stopped by the heroism of Winston Churchill who fought his inner cabinet against negotiating with Hitler at a time when all seemed lost. He was backed up by the heroism of thousands of ordinary citizens, who took their lives in hand to sail their small boats from every little port and inlet across the English Channel to Dunkirk and returned with their cargo of more than 300,000 soldiers who lived to fight another day.

Thus Hitler's revolution was foiled by the heroism of thousands of ordinary citizens. Their heroism, though they did not know it, proved as significant as the lives of the young soldiers whom they saved and spirited back to England under a foggy sky.

One of the most important issues we will have as we build this commons and define the emerging global culture by which we all will live, will be to name the villains and celebrate the heroes who embody the new ideals of human decency, nobility and compassion. By choosing our heroes and our heroines we redefine what the central ethos of our time will be. Indeed, we have heroes and heroines by the thousands from great elders to young amazing children.

Relationships and Partnerships

The key building materials of the Global Commons are not bricks and mortar. Instead, the new building material and energy to build with is made of the stuff of the whole cosmos lodged in the human consciousness of the architects and builders. The things they build—from house to factory to great halls to monuments—are made of the networks between us. Relationships, electronic and personal, are the main building material of the new millennium. From them close partnerships and collaboration of every kind will be built. Out of this material policies of trade and inter-denominational and international organizations of every kind will be created.

Peter Russell, writing in the December, 1999 issue of the *Noetic Sciences Review*, asks the question, what if consciousness was not an emergence of other products of evolution but was a primary energy force in its own right. This would force us to reconsider what we can do by shaping human consciousness to evolve in the direction of "goodness," of caring, compassion and service to each other, and of stewardship of our biosphere.

Such consciousness of millions of people would recreate life on this planet in a new evolved way. Such consciousness defining the rules of the Global Commons would enshrine the sacredness and divinity of human life. The villains who try to serve their own purpose against such divine rights would be quickly put in their places, and every effort, from ordinary citizen to president or monarch to raise the level and quality of the lives of their fellows to higher ground, would add to the building of one global society of shining virtue by whatever they did in their own corner of the world.

Acknowledging the Good

To celebrate and acknowledge the good, a global and professional media would not only focus on the villainies we need to know about to prevent atrocities, but also on the thousands of acts of greatness done each day by Earth citizens.

In my own way I have this opportunity by writing the stories of my own Journeys of Second Adulthood, to talk to friends and colleagues and readers far and wide. To all of us I say at this time of great importance: *We have a job to do!* It is a job of the greatest importance for our generation. Regardless of the busyness of our lives, we need to save some time and energy to build the Global Commons, to create its policies, its institutions and laws in the spirit of human decency and goodness. Each of us can contribute to the legacy by the relationships we are willing to foster and nurture in the years ahead.

Looking to the Future

What is important is not what we have done so far, but what we will accomplish in the years ahead.

In our youth, full of hope, optimism, determination and enthusiasm, we planned and worked and created ourselves so far. However many chronological years we have lived, we are all at a new beginning.

We have a job to do. So let's begin.

December, 1999

The World Cultures are in Transition:

The Tide is Turning

As we approach the millennium moment, less than 100 days in the future at this writing, we see "writ large" in the global mainstream culture, a broad cynicism about the state of the world and our nature as a species that fuels a materialist, present-centred grab for whatever this life can provide. The artifacts of our culture from its songs and cinema to terrible genocidal warfare provide "evidence" to the cynical among us that it's a dog-eat-dog world out there. This justifies the intensely competitive, uncompassionate behaviour of the individual.

And yet. . . to those whose hearts are attuned to the pulse of our species, another picture emerges. It reveals our nobility, our soaring intelligence, and our extraordinary compassion for one another in the most terrible of conditions.

Fifty years ago in a war that took 50 million people, a holocaust of six million ordinary citizens, from old grandmothers and new born infants to budding scientists, gifted doctors, and talented musicians—people of every kind and condition—took place in secret. Leaders from the Pope to Prime Ministers who knew what was happening looked the other way, or colluded in directing the hapless victims to the cattle cars and the crematoria. Boatloads of refugees were turned back from our own shores to their certain deaths.

Today the worst of such atrocities cannot happen. Similar tragedies from Bosnia to Kosovo to East Timor receive worldwide attention and response. The conscience of citizens from many nations and their willingness to act, makes the kind of holocaust experienced in the first half of the 20th century impossible.

The Tide is Turning

At the cusp of the millennium every nation has a ministry to advocate for the environment, and in the most advanced countries the destruction of old growth forests, the pollution of our air, our oceans and our land, does not go on in silence, as cohorts of concerned citizens take up the singular battles of their own causes— the whales, the old-growth forests, the watersheds, etc. News stories now include new thrusts towards making business involved in the production of products like cars, refrigerators and computers also responsible for the cost of recycling these materials as part of the privilege of their sale. While this is still far from the law, it removes the secrecies involved in profit for business without concern for the real cost to society.

In the pursuit of better health, millions of people worldwide are availing themselves of alternative therapies, whose value to recovery and well-being can no longer be kept secret by powerful lobbies or bureaucracies. Religions, which were once isolated towers of exclusive rights to ultimate truth are meeting in inter-denominational congresses designed to promote tolerance of each other's beliefs. Rights to religious freedom are entrenched in the constitutions of all democratic nations. Even justice, long a prerogative of individual nations, has moved into the international court at The Hague, so that leaders who perpetrate evil doing in their nation can no longer do so in secrecy, or without the threat of international redress.

We Are Listening—and Ready to Act

The fact that these issues are exposed by a dogged international media, admittedly intent on profit and sensationalism, is nevertheless possible only because hundreds of millions of citizens are listening worldwide, and some are willing to act. From humanitarian aid, to soldiering on the ground, to quick response teams for earthquake rescue (even from enemy countries) to the millions of local responses to hunger, to poverty, to children's rights, citizens from many countries, from every walk of life, respond to the needs and calls for help. In the face of the most terrible tragedies, the human spirit worldwide celebrates the rescue of a small child trapped for three days under the rubble of an earthquake.

The World Cultures Are in Transition

While it is true that in many places citizen responses are coming from the margins of their major culture, they are now coming from too many places, from too many people, to stop their march to the central ethos or value of all cultures. Today, sensitive and sensible leaders of every kind, their hearts listening to the sounds of different drumming, are moving even the most intractable bureaucracies to new places.

Everywhere we are cultures in transition. The older values of the 20th century are making way for intense, transformational change in the 21st. Citizens of the future will be unwilling to accept businesses that don't look after our environment as we are today unwilling to accept a secret genocide.

We Have a Sacred Trust

We, the citizens, the generations now in charge of the world, and especially those in the developed world have a sacred trust, inherited from our ancestors, whose generations often sacrificed a good life in their own time for our reward in our time—we have a sacred trust to provide an equal legacy to the generations who follow us.

We must find a way to look beyond the busyness of our lives to respond. For while the thrust previously described is inevitable, the momentum for destruction and danger is also in the fast forward position. The urgent agenda is to turn the tide for good soon enough to save the quality of life for our children and grandchildren. While there are millions of us out there, we are weaker and slower when our work is fragmented, focused on a single issue, and isolated from the commons.

Our own issues are certainly crucial and make enormous

demands on our time and energy, but we must also find the strength and courage to extend ourselves across our specific horizons to find the ways to connect, to partner and collaborate. Indeed, some of us must lead the effort to focus our energy on building the bridges and the networks between us. In this endeavour, every act leverages the agenda of the whole.

Life Has Meaning and Purpose

A flood tide of cynicism washes over our societies creating a resistance to a new spirit because the proponents of cynicism have assumed an underlying meaninglessness to life. What if we assumed life is meaningful, that we are connected to our past and to our future and to each other through some kind of divine destiny, which is for the most part mysterious? What support is there for this position as truth, and how would we behave if it were the truth?

We Need Humility

First it is important to understand that our knowledge of who we are from historical antiquity to our place in the universe, is based on many theories and assumptions, which the discoveries of the time reveal bit by bit. In our time these theories, ideas and beliefs are in a continual state of flux and revision. As the telescopes like Hubble and its future generations train increasingly sophisticated technologies deeper into space, more mysteries than answers are revealed. In a picture of 100 billion galaxies congregating in giant clusters around great yawning voids, where we are a tiny planet in a minor galaxy, we must be humble about what we now know and can see from our limited perspective in the cosmos. Yet, wherever we look, from the tiniest particle of ourselves in a growing fetus to the spiral pictures of the Milky Way Galaxy there are patterns and regularities.

Indeed, we and our consciousness are known to have emerged from the ecosystems of shining galaxies. We and they are made from the ashes of interstellar deaths, and we are made from the same stuff as everything else. At the heart of everything is a mystery so dense and so vast, it will take thousands of generations more to unravel.

New Discoveries

Everywhere scientific searching and inquiry, from examining the remains of the "iceman" found in British Columbia's Tatshenshini Park to newly discovered Egyptian tombs dating earlier than 300 B.C., reveal life and culture as meaningful for the people of the time. Belief in ourselves and our search for spiritual answers may be as ancient as our consciousness itself. Thus, we can as thoughtfully and confidently make assumptions about the ultimate divinity of ourselves and our world, even though to date there is no "scientific" proof by current standards.

The idea that any one group, at any time, came upon the whole truth is the ultimate in human arrogance, regardless through what divine inspiration. It therefore behooves us to be fully tolerant of all beliefs, pieces of truth as they may be, knowing that future generations will discover for themselves new more insightful understanding as the horizons of their knowledge expand, much as the true scientist stands humble in face of the awesome mystery that brought us to this time and to this momentary knowing.

There Are Some Universal Truths

Despite our ultimate ignorance of the whole, we have a good understanding of some unalterable truths. The first is that we are all connected by our common consciousness and genetic inheritance. As we work to care for, collaborate, and serve each other, we do the work of the cosmos. This work is like the law of gravity. It keeps everything from flying apart and makes everything viable. This is true even from the tiniest microcosm to the greatest macrocosm. Thus, if we assume ourselves to be caretakers of a meaningful divine destiny and act as if the above laws are true; if we live to reach out, to serve, to care; if we do this, it creates a quality of life for ourselves we cannot replicate by any material or external source.

....From this another universal truth emerges. *Those who serve others also benefit themselves.* Science already has revealed that those who act in a caring, collaborative, serving way pour the chemistry of health, well-being and wellness into a mind and body nurtured and nourished by such behaviour. From primordial times all life needed to cooperate and collaborate to survive. So, by acting on this assumption, we create a winning strategy for ourselves, for those we serve, for our planet, and for the legacy of pride our generations can pass to our descendants.

We Should Be Inspired by Our Awesome Selves

It behooves us to look at the stars and ourselves in wonder at our nobility, and to take the energy of that wonder as inspiration to do the work needed to turn the major cultural ethos of our time from cynicism and materialism to a tide of action for transformation and progress towards goodness. So enabled and advantaged we can enter the third millennium with confidence that the future we create will be life-giving and rewarding for those who follow us.

October, 1999

Real Progress
The Act of Beginning:

How the World is Changed

This morning getting ready for the privilege of writing my thoughts down for the perusal of friends and colleagues around the world, I read through National Geographic's wonderful volume *"Eyewitness to the 20th Century"* where in story and photograph the camera reveals the major forces that have shaped all of our lives.

The record describes the horrors of war, which reaches wrenchingly into my soul with the 1972 photograph of Vietnamese children running in terrified anguish away from the fiery inferno unleashed by the bombing of their school and village. It describes this alongside the majesty of human discovery and invention. Villain and hero are pictured in the same decade.

Pop stars and politicians stand side by side with happenings firmly etched in my own consciousness—the coming of age at Woodstock, the anti-Vietnam riots, the terrible reality of the death of students at Kent State. These are fixed for me personally in the photograph of a single face, in this case of a young co-ed kneeling over the dead body of a fellow student.

On the next page of this amazing record of human activity, appears the report by scientists Godfrey Hounsfield and Allen MacLeod Cormack of the combination of computers and conventional x-rays, which led to the invention of the CAT Scan (Computerized

Axial Tomography) for which they shared the Nobel prize in 1979. These inventions in turn led to the current flood of technological advances in medicine, and the consequent invention of modern neurological imaging using the PET Scan (Positron Emission Tomography) and MRI (Magnetic Resonance Imaging), which daily provide breakthroughs in the understanding of physical and mental diseases.

What a century this has been! The awful and the evil beside the wonderful, the noble and the heroic, mirrored each year in the big and small events of our times. The juxtaposition of the view of life as cycles and as seasons compared with the view of building progress towards a greater good. On balance, this leads me to exclaim in answer to the question are we making progress—towards a more caring compassionate world where all our children may live their lives in peace, in safety, in better health and in more vigorous well being—to answer, "Yes ! Yes! Yes! Yes!"

The question of how this has been done deserves most careful attention and analysis by those of us concerned with our own and our generation's legacy as we cross the millennial line into the 21st century of seasons and cycles.

We live in a time of intense and continuous change. However, change can be merely different forms of the same thing.

How do we progress towards a future that is better, further away from the scourges of the 20th century, further away from war, from poverty, from sickness, from degradation of the planet, and the despair all this brings? How do we move on towards the light of hope, to a truly better, more compassionate world?

The answers lie between the lines in the pages of history that describe the ideas, the acts of nobility, the discoveries and the inventions. They lie in the minds of those willing to dream, to see a vision of a better place, and in the actions taken to create their dreams as reality. In the 20th century, in countries where women have become more equal than at any time in known history, their place was won a piece at a time by their forebears, the suffragettes, the feminists, and the millions of heroic and competent women who just went out every day and did the job in the schools, in the hospitals, in the laboratories, and in the board rooms of business and politics across the nations.

The discoveries in science and technology, in medicine, in physics and engineering, and the making of the laws and policies that govern a compassionate country like Canada, were all achieved in the same way. Reality is wrought from dream to creative vision, and through dogged, determined, courageous action that persists until the reality is established as commonplace, as an accepted part of the culture which becomes the platform for the next steps.

Between the racism of the first half of this century, through Martin Luther King's "I have a dream" to the acceptance of a multicultural diverse society of the late 20th century, lie thousands of acts of courage—from riding the segregated buses of the south to the marches for civil rights, to the daily demonstrations of competence by people of every colour and creed. Events move on, even from the terrible anti-ethnic Holocaust to the present, when a NATO alliance of old enemies is formed to move against those who would perpetrate ethnic cleansing.

Of course, none of this is perfect, and those who find legitimate fault in these imperfections look despairingly at the future. I, on the other hand, choose to see the progress we make, and I choose as mentors, models and heroines those who act to create this progress.

Which brings me to the point of this writing. What is it that we as individuals can do in our time to create a legacy of ongoing progress towards a better, safer, healthier life on a healthy planet? My personal answer lies in the magic of beginning, of taking time to see what needs to be done, of matching these needs to the talents and resources at hand, of describing the vision, of searching out the allies, the colleagues and the fellow conspirators who will enlarge and anchor the vision, and who are willing to take the first steps, from nowhere to somewhere, on the journey to create the new piece of that better future.

In this past year the Institute for Ethical Leadership, itself a new creation just 18 months old, embarked on its first venture called *Connections One: Creating a Web of Good Work*. In playing a part to coordinate this event, I was struck by two kinds of responses from those invited. One kind was to say, "Oh, this is a new thing. . . It has no track record... Who is involved? . . Let me know about the next one. . If it survives, I might be interested. . ." Another response was, "What an exciting idea! How can we contribute? How can we participate?" Of course, it is this latter attitude that makes the next part possible, and it is this willingness to trust one's own contributions and the potential of those willing to act in the first place that allows anything at all to take place, to take form and to grow towards hope for a better future.

The longest part of the journey, the most difficult and demanding in courage and tenacity comes in the first few steps from nowhere to somewhere. However, having reached the first way station on the journey, and having succeeded in creating the energy, the magic and the momentum engendered by a first success, the real test begins.

It is hard to see where success may lead, but the expanded vision creates unlimited new possibilities and opportunities all around. Though the idea is still fragile and needs much improvement and expanded participation, it now has the magic of momentum. It is somewhere, somewhere new and exciting. It is in a place which did not exist before, and which now has a true reality. It is also a lesson, an example, a lighthouse for each participant on how to begin something new. It will provide lessons for those who help it survive, succeed and grow.

Margaret Mead's anthropological mind, one of the best of this century, told us that a few determined and committed people, rallying around an idea, a vision, a dream, can change their world for the better. At the end of the 20th century and the beginning of the new millennium, human society is more capable than ever in its history. At the same time, the need for a competent response from citizen leaders everywhere has never been more urgent.

As the summer begins, I see a groundswell of responses for good work in every corner and crevice of the planet. I am thus encouraged to rest, enjoy and store energy for the next steps on my own journey. I wish all of you the same. Let the journeys we take be fruitful and full of the enduring joy of friendship, collegiality and good spirit.

July, 1999

Relationships

It is widely believed in our culture that wealth creates the happy circumstances that bring the good life. But truly, wealth only buys your place at the table described above. It provides the food, but not the appetite; the fun of being in such a place, but not the joy in the experience. It buys acquaintances, but not friends; leisure, but not peace. In other words, the depth of the experience bought simply by wealth is thin and transitory. The next day we are the same. The soul continues in winter and spring does not really come, even though the weather and seasons change.

Emotional Intelligence and the New Way to be Smart:

Building Quality Relationships

Spring seeps into our winter's soul to produce a vitality and a focus on newness, youthfulness, birth and rebirth. For me it brings a renewed sense of purpose along with new ideas and fresh projects. This spring, Desmond and I spent several days on Salt Spring Island, one of the jewels of the Gulf Islands which we are blessed to have close at hand in this part of the world. Each morning our hosts at a bed and breakfast hideaway presided over a gloriously set table, displaying their culinary artistry to perfection. Here we joined six other guests to eat and chat about the weather and good places and sights to see, after which we went on our separate ways to enjoy the day.

Thinking about this, I am moved to say that *much of life is like a bed and breakfast*. We meet, we talk very superficially, and we go on our way. No one is affected or changed in any way by the conversation. Moments later it is as if nothing had been said at all.

What then does affect us, change us, move us to feel and think deeply, cause growth and progress? What does create a meaningful and "juicy" life?

It is widely believed in our culture that wealth creates the happy circumstances that bring the good life. But truly, wealth only buys your place at the table described above. It provides the food, but not the appetite; the fun of being in such a place, but not the joy in the experience. It buys acquaintances, but not friends; leisure, but not peace. In other words, the depth of the experience bought simply by wealth is thin and transitory. The next day we are the same. The soul continues in winter and spring does not really come, even though the weather and seasons change.

For those of us seeking to make a difference, the "bed and breakfast" approach to life presents a dilemma. We know it is not enough, but we don't quite know how to break free. The reasons sit side by side with the answers. Both are grounded in who we are as a species.

We are emotional creatures. From birth mothers nurture their children with their *emotional rationality.* This is not a contradiction in terms. Mothers *know* that it is the quality of emotional nurturing which determines a child's psychological health or weakness. Moreover, it is the extent of the father's support (emotional as much as material) of the mother and child that will contribute significantly to the growing family's strength or distress in later years.

The child who is emotionally strong is the one who enters school confident and ready to learn, curious and open to the continuing newness and awe the educational system can provide. Alternatively, if emotional security is not there, the school experience becomes fearful and the child takes away only a thin layer of skills in language, reading and arithmetic. All too often, this is the common school experience our young people take into the world as adults.

Thus, emotional rationality develops the confidence derived from being loved and valued. It underlies all the developing intelligences from cognitive to social and personal and cannot be separated from them. Indeed, it fuels and motivates every kind of learning. Because we are genetically designed to be emotional, our internal environment, especially the immune system, becomes the container into which everything else is poured throughout our entire life.

We therefore cannot separate our emotions from our cognitive growth and the development of all of our experience and expertise. Nor can we truly understand or measure or make predictions about our intellect as separate from our emotions, anymore than we can truly understand fish outside of the water of their river or ocean. It is the emotional confidence and courage that determines the success and the depth of our learning, right from the beginning, and it continues to mediate our performance to the end.

This means that the development of cognitive intelligence which often determines our material success is dependent on the kind and quality of our relationships, for it is through relationships that our belief system, our values, or how we see the world, develops, deepens and grows.

Our experiences mediated by relationships are what change us. They move us to growth, and to act with courage or fear as we confront life's challenges. It is in these relationships that our intelligence, our passion for life, our sensitivities and our purpose develop.

As a person who has spent a full professional career measuring and mediating cognitive growth and achievement, I have often been called on to answer the question why some children succeed and others with the same cognitive ability fail. To answer, we often misuse the term "motivation" suggesting that some are motivated to succeed while others are "lazy." Yet, I can honestly say I have never met a child or adult who had the survival skills in school of reading and math who did not use them because of laziness.

In fact, it appears that there is an underlying emotional confidence which determines the outcome for particular children. Over a lifetime of academic experience, emotional intelligence mediated on a daily basis by relationships in the classroom with teachers and peers, is what determines the learning climate for the individual child. In turn, this affects the willingness to try and, as a consequence, the achievement—all, of course, within the cognitive potential of the child.

It is not surprising, therefore, that IQ, a measure of cognitive ability, predicts so little of the life outcome for the individual. We have known this for many years from our studies of correlations between IQ and life success, but up until recently as psychologists and teachers we had very little to offer by way of answer. Finally, in the 1990s a new concept introduced by Daniel Goleman called *Emotional Intelligence* begins to get at what truly determines life success. In two recent books (*Emotional Intelligence*, 1995 and *Working with Emotional Intelligence*, October 1998) Goleman describes the new ways of being smart as inclusive of the qualities of self-awareness, self-control, empathy, and the skills of listening, resolving conflict and co-operating with others. All of these qualities are nurtured by relationships.

In his books Goleman identifies the brain structures deep within us that define us and moderate our responses to our experiences with others and the world. In these scientific explanations based on the important recent understandings derived from co-operative research in many disciplines from molecular genetics to neurobiology and neuropsychology, a whole new process of the measurement of intelligence, achievement and leadership is emerging based on the ideas of emotional competence.

Goleman's *Framework* includes personal competencies such as self-confidence, initiative, trustworthiness, and optimism as well as social competence, especially empathy. All these are qualities that depend for growth on the depth and quality of relationships.

So a new dialogue is beginning in the area of personal development. Which brings me back to my thoughts of spring and the wonder of nature and to the way we live our lives either as a bed and breakfast or as a journey where we go deep to be passionate, willing to enter into meaningful relationships with others and to care for and be cared for by them.

Such a way of living opens us to the bigger picture of our humanity—its past, present and potential future. It produces the purpose to grow, to evolve to a wiser more mature place, to enjoy deeply, to breathe in the spring, and to leave a legacy for the future worthy of our descendants.

Such living creates the opportunity to reach out, to reach across the borders and barriers between us and to build the connections, the bridges, the networks and the forums where our relationships and our humanity may grow and flourish. May more and more of us find one another in these wholesome spaces which lie beyond the material comforts that wealth on its own is able to provide; and in this meeting may we do the work together so desperately needed to bring out the best, the most noble of our qualities.

Let us develop our emotional rationality in the next centuries as we developed our cognitive abilities in the past. Such a legacy can only produce the wisdom and the maturity needed for a future in which all our children and grandchildren can safely and happily live.

April, 1999

Relationships, Partnerships and Alliances:

The Energy Source That Can Save the Planet

The early days of a new year present a brand new canvas on which to paint. What images, what masterpieces will emerge from the easels of humanity in the 366 days ahead that will impact the six billion of us now inhabiting this extraordinary, wonderful, yet seemingly besieged planet?

The artist begins with an array of colours on a palette and with images and intentions in mind. What is produced from these possibilities is unique to the mind and skill of each artist. Even though exactly the same colours, brushes and canvas are used, no two paintings will be alike.

Each artist paints for some audience so at least one other, and possibly millions, can see the results of her feelings, thoughts and, of course, skills. In the same way, journalists, photographers, film makers and story tellers present their work to a world where only a very few are chosen for the masses to see. Importantly, all the pictures and works exist, each just as real, and often just as skillfully executed as those chosen for wider consideration.

We are, however, duped into thinking that what is selected is somehow the most important, the best, or even all there is, and most people give no thought to the billions of other images and stories that simultaneously exist and affect the future of lives often in much more profound and powerful ways than what we are led to understand is the news and reality of our times. Indeed, what is judged to be news is usually the aberrations, the strange or the bizarre, and the billions of stories that portray the norm are left untold or relegated to the back pages.

Because of the assumption that human beings only really pay attention when shocked by the "badness," the violence, the darkness of others, media leaders from editors to film makers have perpetrated the grossest of great lies. Everything they choose about the worst that human beings can do or imagine creates by their publicity a fabric of our darkest trends allowing light to poke through here and there, often only for comic relief.

Strangely, this serves an important, though usually unintended, purpose. It stimulates the good minds to go to work on addressing some of the worst situations, and solutions come forward in billions of individual actions and products that actually keep the planet flourishing with life and light and hope, promoting progress towards a kinder, more civil, more compassionate global society than we know.

Some Technological Breakthroughs

Let me explain by example. The great created disasters of the 2003 canvas are well known. We know the huge toll in human life and well-being taken by the AIDS, EBOLA and SARS viruses, and by the toxins and pollutants spewed into the air and water of the planet by the actions of the global industrial and military machines, and by the threat of possible use of nuclear and other weapons of mass destruction by any nation that possesses them. We know this because these things and others equally distressing fill the headlines and the news bites. But how much do we know about other initiatives that can be a counteracting force?

For example, do we know:

- that at the University of Massachusetts Medical School researchers Craig Mello and Andrew Fire of the Carnegie Institute of Washington discovered how a kind of RNA disrupts the genetic code of viruses so they are unable to reproduce? This breakthrough earned them the Wiley Prize with the electrifying implications of future treatment of viral disease.

- that researchers at the US Army Medical Research Institute in Maryland appear to have created an effective vaccination for the horrifying EBOLA virus, which kills up to 80% of those infected?

- that in South Africa Lynette Denny, gynecologist and obstetrician, was funded by the Bill and Melinda Gates Foundation and named her country's woman scientist of the year for ground breaking studies in developing low cost alternatives for preventing cervical cancer in countries that can't afford the pap smear, which has the potential to save the lives of hundreds of thousands of women in the developing world?

- that the on the ground strategies in Canada and around the world of effectively controlling the spread of SARS prevented further deaths of potentially millions, while searches for identifying tests, treatments and vaccines are meeting with exciting success in preparation for the potential re-emergence of the disease?

- that at an annual breast cancer symposium American scientists unveiled a nuclear camera capable of identifying tumours the size of a pin head long before a lump can be felt or detected with present mammography. Eventually this technology is intended to spot the subtle chemical signatures that signal malignancy developing at the cellular level, potentially saving millions of women's lives through early diagnosis and treatment?

Can you imagine the potential of the lives saved by these initiatives, what they would contribute to the prosperity of their countries over decades, not to mention the contributions of their descendants?

Those of us following the current degradation of the planet by carbon-based fuels and the over use of energy could be in perpetual despair, if we did not know that:

- in California scientists are exploring the nanotechnology potential of photovoltaics and the possibility of creating building materials or even a paint that could convert sunlight into electricity. Can you imagine energy emerging from painted surfaces all around the planet, even in poor countries, instead of having to build and support mammoth energy projects, nuclear plants, pipelines and all the potential damage to the planet that they create?

- in Austria a research team has found a way to mimic the chemicals produced by amorous glow worms creating a thin foil that generates light when stimulated by the tiniest electrical charge. Can you imagine how when attached to fabric or other material this discovery could produce light even in the most remote parts of the world?

- in America a new technology is developing using the energy efficient light emitting diode that already illuminates computers, cell phones and some traffic lights and that could mean the end of the power hungry light bulb, replacing fluorescent, incandescent and halogen bulbs, saving billions in energy costs and reducing the need to burn fossil fuels.

Indeed, without fanfare all over the planet using the carbon free energy from the wind, the sun and the tides and eventually the limitless dark energy in space, experiments and discoveries continue, many of which will be painted on the waiting canvas of 2004.

While the inventions, discoveries and breakthroughs reported above are only the tiniest proportion of the progress in 2003, they have one important phenomenon in common. Their potential outcome is systemic with the possibility of really making an "on the ground" difference in the extraordinarily complex fabric of the economies and even cultures of the future of the planet.

A New Form of Leadership

Side by side with the technological breakthroughs comes another important development, a new form of leadership, emerging in our time with subtle but very real signs of it everywhere. A new brand of creative activism is developing that goes well beyond attention getting marches and protests, which in the early part of the 20th century were the means of obtaining civil rights, securing the vote for the disenfranchised and achieving labour rights. Even now this form of activism is being used to draw attention to global wrong doing and to overthrow dictators. But we have to move on.

Adolescent societies growing towards adulthood of compassionate concern for their citizens needed that kind of massive participation. But underlying this turmoil and what the media report as reality is a growing army of concerned citizens worldwide who have much greater issues to worry about. For life across the whole interconnected planet is now at risk, and this requires a more strategic and emotionally intelligent human response. Millions of leaders need to move the world's economies and cultures on from compassion for its citizens' rights and health to wisdom that embraces the need to preserve the environment on which we all depend for life, and to do this in such a way that we can support and sustain in health a growing population with all their accompanying needs.

Moreover, there is a great urgency to do this. We do not have the luxury of time of hundreds of years to develop the consciousness in all the citizens of the planet that would lead to good outcome through literacy and the education systems. We have to act now to prevent global destruction. New technologies alone are not enough. There must be political and social will to embrace new ways of living on the planet.

Thus a new kind of leadership needs to emerge around the world that understands that the most important energy source on the planet is not oil, or nuclear power, or the natural forces of wind, sun and water, or even the extraordinary nanotechnology described above. **No, the most important energy source available and ready for use is the power of human relationships among those in positions to make systemic change and those with the creative ideas to understand how to proceed to make a real future difference.**

To do this, alliances, partnerships and collegial friendships need to be fostered among all kinds of unlikely people, even those formerly considered enemies. Activists and inventors need to create alliances with corporate executives and politicians of every stripe to change the way we do the business of our daily life. And the storytellers must be prominent in the mix, telling the new stories, presenting the new visions that are needed to change the culture and the consciousness of humanity to understand our underlying connections as one human species within the great biosphere of all life.

Examples in Action

Scandinavian countries, whose economies are among the most stable and buoyant of the OECD (Organization for Economic Cooperation and Development), are leading the way. One method is the concept of *tax-shifting* (that is, tax the bad things in society and give the breaks to those who contribute the good things). This is especially effective when used as a response to global climate change. Research backed up by some 2600 economists including eight Nobel Laureates supports this approach.

In Canada, Donna Morton from British Columbia, has earned a rare Ashoka Fellowship for her passion and innovative thinking around tax shifting. She describes this concept as the single most important lever we can pull to address climate change, environmental pollution and energy consumption. She has already met with Prime Minister Paul Martin and New Democratic Party Leader, Jack Layton. She has founded her "think-and-do tank" called the Centre for Integral Economics, and has worked with Winnipeg Mayor, Glen Murray in the creation of a New Deal agenda, which includes the use of Municipal tax shifting with consumption based fees and fines.

Morton, who admits to having been a self righteous angry student activist (she once chained herself to an oil drilling vessel), learned through experience on committees with executives that the issues were incredibly complex. She determined to be part of a "brokerage of relationships," where she could get close to people who can and would effect change. She is already making a strategic difference where the outcome might be a better environment in which to live and grow for all Canadians.

By extension, can you imagine a worldwide use of this concept, especially in the US, where producers of toxins and pollutants have to pay for the real cost of their product including the environmental cost, while the producers of energy creating paint, or energy saving diodes, or natural energy products are promoted, sponsored and endorsed by the good economics of delivering their products to the masses?

Indeed, such a project is already underway in Canada, driven by another Ashoka award recipient. In Tofino, British Columbia, Nicole Rycroft has created a non-profit marketing initiative that has changed the face of book publishing in Canada. A coalition between the friends of Clayoquot Sound, Greenpeace and the BC Chapter of the Sierra Club of Canada was the force behind the decision of Raincoast Books to print its titles, most notably J.K. Rowling's *Harry Potter and the Order of the Phoenix,* on ancient-forest-friendly, 100 percent, post-consumer recycled paper.

This coalition initiative contacts book publishers around the world and educates them about how much of the world's paper comes from ecologically diverse forests. They are asked to phase out paper coming from ancient growth forests. (Almost 40 percent of Canada's ancient temperate rainforests and 65 percent of Canadian boreal forests are logged to produce paper).

With a vision to allow mass producers of paper products to print on ancient-forest-friendly paper, Rycroft has brokered *relationships* between printers, paper mills, book publishers and even authors. She created an advertising campaign with the risqué slogan "Who's good between the covers?" showing Canadian literary heavyweights Margaret Atwood, Timothy Findley, Pierre Berton, Alice Munroe and Austin Clarke in bed.

After only three years, with only two part time employees, Rycroft's Markets Initiative has seen a shift in the book publishing industry from a situation where none of the printers had ancient-forest-friendly paper available, to the current state where 67 publishers in Canada have commitments to shift away from or eliminate the use of papers from ancient forests. Eight printers now stock these papers and paper mills have developed eight new types of paper. Publishers indicate that printing flagship titles on 100 percent recycled paper is the kind of publicity that can't be bought. Here, too, we see a perfect example of how leadership of a new kind, was able to broker relationships with the power to create the needed change while producing an outstanding economic advantage for those who participated.

Again, let us extend the vision. Can you imagine a world in which the ingredients for paper are grown as a crop and the forests worldwide saved from cutting are used for parks and adventure tourism and are harvested for their pharmacological and health benefits?

Thus, the power to change the world and to save its environment and culture is currently available both in terms of potential relationships, partnerships and alliances, and the growing technological creativity to serve our needs in a wholesome, healthful and economically sustainable way. To do this many more initiatives and the creative leadership to foster, endorse and spearhead the breakthroughs in every field need to be encouraged.

Looking Ahead

With these thoughts I face the new canvas of 2004 with hope and enthusiasm for what the new and emerging leadership these alliances of citizens, professionals, entrepreneurs, scientists, business people, politicians, bureaucrats, artists and writers worldwide may create. What is needed is what artists always need: **a vision profoundly and deeply imagined so that they may create its reality.**

Thus, for me 2004 is a year that requires Big Dreams and Visions of a future we will be proud to leave as legacy to the generations that follow. Considering the millions already working, the task will demand the qualities of courage, initiative and imagination. The future is pregnant with these awesome possibilities.

January, 2004

A Vision of Hope
for a Culture of Wisdom

The first summer of the 21st century produces a paradox of peace and tension that creates the dual experience for thoughtful citizens of hope and despair taken in a single breath. Global warming or other factors make parts of the world hot enough to kill. The fragile peace so desperately strived for in Ireland seems to be falling apart. Suicide bombers and military retaliation keep the violence flowing red in the Middle East.

Yet elsewhere the signs of summer abound. Health and enjoyment surround the everyday North American experience as we dine in outdoor restaurants in our millions, enjoy picnics, swim and go boating, gather for festivals of song, sport and fireworks, travel and celebrate at home, on beaches, in parks and in wilderness places.

It is the very complexity of this single breath, these multiple contrasting images, these split screens of activity, that present the great challenge of our time. We are called to reach a different level of consciousness, one that understands we do not live in simple times, one that tolerates the complexity and yet sees beyond to solutions and discoveries that are elegant, straightforward and effective.

At issue is the need to honour and respect a different kind of intelligence. It is a quality as old as our origins, and it is newly developing in millions in our time. It demands as a beginning a high order of cognitive ability, especially a language skill capable of understanding and expressing complex ideas. It calls for a mind-frame that can see the big picture, synthesize disparate elements and invent new solutions. Yet, even this is no longer enough.

Today's challenge demands a deep and great compassion for oneself and for the world. It requires a recognition of feeling, of intuitive understanding, a great self-awareness and the ability for self-discipline and self-control. It calls for the ability to lead others to respect and to calmness, even in moments of high emotion and stress. These combinations of qualities are now being called Emotional Intelligence.

Emotional Intelligence

Described first in 1990 by Salovey and Mayer and expanded and delineated by Daniel Goleman, this body of work underlines the importance of these competencies on performance in the workplace. Goleman has written three books on the subject, *Emotional Intelligence* (1995), reissued as the 10th Anniversary edition in 2005, *Working with Emotional Intelligence* (1998) and *The Emotionally Intelligent Workplace* (2001). Through this work and that of others, new attention is being directed to training and development in emotional competence.

However, it is the identification of the primacy of these skills and personal qualities as critical for harmony and success in human relations in general, that will lead in the decades that follow to the new respect and honour for these abilities that will be needed to evolve consciousness of many millions to the level needed for the creation of peace and compassionate civil society in our time.

New scientific discovery about the centrality of emotion in brain function through brain imaging technologies is providing information and explanation of the power of the combination of high order cognitive *and* emotional intelligence.

Imagine an incident that creates explosive responses in the workplace, the international arena, or even the family. For a fraction of a second before the participants in the process are aware of their own experience and intention to act, the brain reacts to the information provided by the situation by flooding the body with the chemistry of stress. This physical phenomenon now escalates across the milliseconds as awareness and then judgment produces a torrent of chemical responses. With this chemical soup now swirling in our bloodstream, we respond to these physical sensations and perceived emotions (such as fear, anger, rage or exhilaration) with the rapid short cut habitual actions or schemas first learned in infancy and consolidated in adolescence and adulthood.

In families and societies where children observe and learn to model violence as a typical response, explosive incidents produce a situation which is out of control within a second or two. This is especially so if more than one participant in the incident also responds in this way, and if there is no one in the area to calm the process down.

In cultures where there is no sense of safety and where fear is rampant, one can easily see why violence prevails as such a common response. Understanding this can easily lead us to despair, except that this is only part of the story.

Explanations from Science

Another whole set of factors need to be considered. To do this, let us return to the explanations provided by science. Matter, long considered permanent and real, now turns out to be both impermanent and ephemeral, especially the matter of living organisms like human beings. Matter is made up of molecules, which are made up of atoms, which are made up of particles and waves, which at the foundation (as far as we know) turns out to be energy. At this energetic level enormous complexity, flow and change occur in milliseconds. At the point of human awareness, mindful intent by one of the people in the drama to interrupt the habitual responses of the participants can calm or reinterpret the situation to provide time for rational thinking to occur.

It is as if in the midst of great confusion you are flying through a bank of clouds to emerge on the other side to clear blue sky. Here wisdom, good sense and human nobility can take over, and the situation can produce a whole different outcome. Such mindfulness, such clarity of thinking, is the very essence of emotional intelligence. These qualities of self-awareness and self-control allow for a perspective of empathy and service towards others that leads to visionary leadership producing outcomes of co-operation and collaboration

Thus the new recognition of the value of these qualities and new respect and honour for those who practice these competencies can be the first step in introducing the training in this mindfulness to millions of others. Just as the recognition of the economic value of literacy and numeracy led to universal education in Western culture, so the understanding of the value of high order emotional intelligence, which includes cognitive intelligence, will lead to new process of training at every level where education takes place.

Two Important Demographic Issues

It is also important to recognize that there already exists within every community and culture emotionally competent and wise individuals who intuitively understand right action. Never before in the history of humanity have there been so many. This is due to two important demographic issues. First, wisdom of the kind described above takes time to develop, especially when it is not always fostered by the culture. The increased and increasing life span of citizens worldwide throughout the 20th century means there are more elders who have had a life span long enough to learn these skills in every facet of community life.

Second, these skills are the natural heritage of women, who as the producers and nurturers of life have learned the skills of peace-making at their mother's knee. The new honor and respect to these ingrained skills provides opportunities in the workplaces and boardrooms of the world for the viewpoint and exercise of this feminine perspective. As women achieve leadership places across the society and as this perspective is seen to have important economic as well as cultural value, they will grow in number and importance, and their way of thinking will affect the whole culture.

Just as the number of "cultural creatives" identified by Paul Ray and Sherri Anderson have become hundreds of millions worldwide, so the cohorts of emotionally competent men and women will become hundreds of millions. Moreover, while the earlier group took almost two full generations to emerge, the current speed of change will produce this new result much faster.

Hope for a New Time

Can you imagine what will happen in the world's explosive places and in the societies, communities and families where people are mindful about the responses that could lead to violent outcomes? Peace, respect, right action and higher consciousness will be the result of a consciousness evolution, a growth and development towards qualities of wisdom.

The complexity, confusion and despair that come from the observation in our time that explosive and negative outcomes prevail, also contain the clarity and elegance and hope of a new time for humanity. It is important to hold the vision in the midst of the clouds that there is blue sky ahead.

August, 2001

Intelligence and Consciousness: Two Separate Systems?

The Forrest Gump Phenomenon

Cartesian duality, now in growing disrepute, sees the mind and brain as completely separate entities. The critics of this view see a full and total integration of mind and body as a starting place for understanding human behaviour. Which view is right? The truth may turn out to be in another place, or be somewhere along the continuum between both points of view.

We know the brain is a non-local organ; that is, while sited in the head it sends its messengers, its neuropeptides, into every cell of the body. Here, at the quantum level, microtubules wait with ready hands to receive the messages and turn them into signals for body function, for thinking and behaviour.

What we recognize and measure as intelligence may be the simpler interaction between the brain and its genetic physical heritage. Consciousness, on the other hand, (which includes mind and what we refer to as the soul, spirit, free will, etc.) may transcend this form of interaction, and at the quantum level (of atomic components of matter) embrace a complex organization of psycho-physical phenomena. We do not yet have the technical capacity to see this. However, from the theoretical and observational phenomena there is much evidence that has not yet filtered through the margins between science and mysticism. There are many examples of situations in which the intelligence is limited, yet what we call the spirit is enormously powerful. This may be a case in which the brain itself either through injury or disease delivers a simple intelligence, but consciousness transcends it in the form of evolved human behaviour.

The film, *Forrest Gump*, is a profound illustration of this phenomenon. The main character has a simple intelligence. He is considered stupid by many others. He fails to see such complex phenomena as "double entendre" or sarcasm. He does not see through deception. To Gump a promise is a promise. He displays the qualities of an evolved mind. Beyond the egocentric, he cares in the fullest sense for those to whom he extends friendship. This includes saving his fallen comrades in battle; or attacking a man, without concern for his own danger, who slaps his girlfriend ("You shouldn't have hit her," he says); or keeping a promise to his dead friend by giving large sums of money to his friend's family because his own good fortune has come from an idea they were meant to share. Further, he demonstrates how easy it is to get into a state of flow when his life's mission is focused and directed by a laser-like simplicity. He gains fame in football by his prowess as a runner. He wins a medal for bravery by going back again and again to save his fallen comrades in war. He becomes a ping-pong champion. He achieves fame and fortune, yet it doesn't change his simple purposes. He is entirely uncritical of others and extends a life-giving friendship to those who offer him a seat on the bus, and a place in their hearts, while others ridicule and reject him for his "stupidity."

Forrest Gump, besides being a wonderfully inspirational movie, shows that while brain function may produce a limited intelligence, the consciousness that transcends it may be free to evolve into a more magnificent form. Thus, it is possible that two systems exist together in the same human being, one at the presently observable level of communication between brain and cell, and the other at the more complex quantum level of consciousness. Both systems are physical and potentially measurable at some future time.

In some cases, while the first system may be damaged or limited by circumstance, the second may be free to achieve its evolved potential. If this is so, we should not necessarily weigh human stature by "cleverness," nor should we be so quick to judge potential human contribution by numbers on an I.Q. test.

February, 1995

Wisdom

The genetic pool of people in every nation bent on supporting life strengthens the adaptive, creative and wise response. It is this cohort who will ultimately prevail and win the war. In the future their influence and their genes will survive in every community where the struggle takes place.

therefore...

We must act with sustained courage and perseverance against those who act against life, knowing that the history of the "goodness" of our species is at least as long as the stories of our wars, our cruelty and our ferocity.

A Wisdom Essay for an Evolving Humanity

Homo Sapiens Sapiens: Our New Story

This summer, in Portland, Oregon, at an exhibit of Egyptian antiquities I touched the dark grey stone of an animal goddess carved 5000 years ago. Sitting enthroned, majestic and full of grace, this creation, with the body of a woman and head of a lioness, moved me to touch the deep roots of my own humanity. Many questions followed: Who are we, truly? Where did we come from? Why have we been so violent? How could such grace and peace as carved in this statue so long ago co-exist with this history of violence? Why are we changing now? Where are we going? Can we plan the journey and decide on the destination?...

Also this summer, the reading of many books and articles put new thoughts and ideas on the table: *How the Irish Saved Western Civilization* and *The Gift of the Jews* by Thomas Cahill, *Conscious Evolution* by Barbara Marx Hubbard, and others. As well as the research into antiquity, I am continuously considering changing world views and scientific responses to some of the above questions.

The most recent research confirms that as a modern species, we emerged as recently as 100,000 years ago out of Africa and spread across the world. At that point there was great uniformity in the way we lived in small groups, probably only ten to twenty thousand such communities. The way we supported our survival was by hunting and gathering in our local habitats. While other hominid groups, like the Neanderthals in northern Europe, co-existed with us, the major difference between us and them was our ability with language. Early in this hundred thousand year history, language was simple and likely limited to the description of the world as we knew it then. As time went by, these languages became increasingly diverse, developing along with the different cultures and traditions of these small groups. Our genetic roots, only different by eight base pairs in a 379 base strip of DNA, had the built-in capacity for speech that enabled our initial survival. By 40,000 years ago the cousins of African heritage had spread across the Eurasian continent with bands of travelers slipping across frozen seas, land bridges and easily navigable water, to become the indigenous populations of everywhere. These ancients took their relatively simple language and ways of life into modern times wherever they have been present on Earth. As we are now discovering, only a few built complex civilizations.

Meanwhile, some of them spread across the Eurasian continent, where no substantial geographic feature prevented their migration, and where a similar climate, topography and soil allowed for the continuation of their way of life. Mostly cut off from one another, except for other bands in their locality with whom they competed, they became the uniquely diverse cultural racial and linguistic groups we meet when currently known history begins some 10,000 years ago.

By this time, the growing communities were fiercely protective of insiders, the life blood of their future, and particularly aggressive towards the outsiders with whom they competed for place and advantage. Long ago they had likely eliminated such competitors as the Neanderthals wherever they found them, as well as weaker breeds of their own species.

By 10,000 years ago, new technology, especially that related to the control of the animals they hunted and the plants they gathered, allowed them to live in larger and larger groups with more time to invest in creativity and better ways to support larger groups. This both facilitated and required more diverse and complex vocabulary. Further, it required planning for the future, which demanded a more sophisticated higher order thinking we call abstract thinking.

Wherever technology, geography and climate produced greater abundance in nutritional support, more survived, and in the places where more gathered in relative abundance and safety, such as in the Middle East and in the Tigris and Euphrates valley, abstract language and vocabulary increased. In this way the thought and ideas and inventions in every field, from spiritual concepts to engineering, to planning and executing conquest, became more and more complex.

Across our history from these early roots, these out of Africa originals, competed with outsiders, conquering and enslaving where they could, and nurturing their own.

Meanwhile, some enclaves, which we have learned about through their mosaics, stone ruins and artifacts, were large and prosperous enough to trade as well as fight with others. To do this, they needed a way to keep records in word and number of objects like cattle, agricultural goods and artifacts; so written language and number systems were invented, which in turn accelerated enormously their ability to think and plan. From these abilities Asia's great civilizations were built, in ancient Sumer, Egypt and Canaan, as well as India and China. The abundance and prosperity which their citizens enjoyed enabled them to build great armies and further accelerated the need for invention of higher order language to plan victorious conquests and protect larger and larger empires.

By 5000 years ago, the sculptor who carved the statue I touched came from a civilization where higher order abstract language and thinking enabled citizens to conceive and plan for life after death, at least for a few fortunate ones, and to produce great art and complex bureaucracy, all the while continuing to compete and kill for competitive advantage wherever possible, and at the same time nurturing and protecting their inner communities.

Somehow, in these last 5000 years, sophisticated language and its thinking also produced another strand of ideas. This flowered in particular in the golden age of Greece, 2500 years ago, where outstanding thinkers like Socrates and Plato began to extend the hierarchical power base built for destruction of outsiders to sow the seeds of democracy, of equality of citizenship rights and consequent responsibilities, and a new system of justice. Over the centuries since then, these principles have been given further refinement in the constitutions of all countries whose governance is based on these original concepts and ideals.

In a similar way, spiritual thinking based on language, especially written language, sought to establish for the generations to come, the rules of good conduct, at least among the believers in the inner group, and to tell their histories. These new principles based on respect and love within the inner group became the laws of nations up to our own time.

In modern times, as the principles of conduct in the inner group began to recognize and respect its own citizens of a wider and more diverse nature, including its own women and even descendants of former slaves, society flourished as never before, and the language to describe what was happening again increased in complexity.

Most important, the number of those included in the inner pools who were educated, who could read and write, and who could think critically, abstractly and creatively, increased exponentially. With the inclusion of women this group multiplied manyfold, now including women's unique perspective which leaned towards respect for life, nurturing and equality in relationship with each other and with their men. By the latter half of the 20th century, the predisposition of earlier societies to fight, overtake, compete, dominate, enslave had peaked and was declining from the apex of expression in the terrible violence of the first half of the century. It should always be remembered that it takes a less complex vocabulary and a lower level of thought to kill, than to cooperate, negotiate and plan a better future.

New ideas and new forms of communication are flourishing in our time. Further, the individuals emerging to speak, write and invent with this level of language are vastly increasing in numbers. They include women and the formerly disenfranchised, and they have the tools and means to reach out and connect with each other.

The planetary home of these out of Africa cousins has become a global village, in which their numbers, their ability to invent more and higher order ideas, and their need to cooperate, is impelling the consciousness of this species to evolve again.

It is important to note that over time millions of individual tiny changes result in a picture of evolution as a leap of progress or a major transformation and transcendence. We, the generations alive today, are observing the transcendence of consciousness of many millions of our citizens. This is not to say the change can or should happen all at once. However, the evolution towards more complexity, cooperation and higher order language and thinking is inevitable. What is more, for the first time *the inner group is becoming all of us* and the survival smarts of our antiquity built into our genetic heritage will lead us eventually to nurture all global citizens. More and more, our survival depends on our cooperation, and we will invent the methods to do it, just as our forebears did when the village meant 50 individuals.

What then shall we do about this?

If what I am saying here is accurate, or even partly so, and evolution towards collaboration and peace is the future, those alive today need to recognize this and spread the word. By our actions to improve our own thinking, and by our modeling, mentoring and collaborating with others of like mind, we need to hurry along our journey towards becoming *Homo sapiens sapiens*, a global family who nurture each other, act as stewards to our environment, and consider the greater future of our human descendants.

August, 1998

Why Wisdom Balanced by Intelligence and Creativity Will Win the War Against World Terrorism

Post September 11, 2001:
The Search for Higher Ground

Years of destructive planning by minds warped by hard line primitive views of the nature of human spirit and the divine, culminated in a single day of infamy to change the world forever. The watching world stunned, fear-struck and grief stricken allowed itself for the moment to lose power and so lose the first battle to the dark forces of the instigators of this brutal act of evil. But the war for humanity's future is not won or lost by these singular acts, however many and however brutal. The lessons of history teach that out of the ashes of these individual acts of infamy rises the phoenix of a new and more powerful time.

Why is this so? Why can we be confident that "goodness," meaning life-giving compassion and even wisdom, will prevail, even in the time of our darkest hour?

In the past we have turned to spiritual answers to this question. Through the ages, and even today, responses include the belief that "God" is on the side of goodness and being all powerful and in covenant with humanity will make it so.

Today we can turn to science to provide more clarity through understanding evolutionary principles and their application to the evolution of human consciousness. To go this route we need to understand what intelligence is and how intelligent people create and maintain their environments, whatever their culture. We also need to examine the quality and kind of human thinking we call creativity so that we understand the forces of thought that promote change and evolution, not only of technology and material factors, but also of ideas and consciousness itself.

It will be important also to consider what happens when intelligence and creativity are engaged together in a balanced way to produce a synthesis of the kind of thinking we consider wise.

Finally, we need to apply this perspective to the grand story of the evolutionary journey of all life, and especially human life, to understand how the very nature of life supports those whose activities and cultural imperatives are life-giving and sustaining.

What is intelligence? Virtually all definitions of intelligence see it as *the ability to adapt to the environment.* Intelligent people are those who acquire the skills that lead to their fitting into existing environments. These skills lead to whatever reward society provides. In Western civilization the acquisition of these skills lead to success in education, especially post-secondary education, technical and professional expertise, business success, status, power and money. In a changing society those who adapt best to the changes adopted by the mainstream do the best.

Creativity is different. Definitions of creativity say that it is *the ability to produce ideas and products that are both high in quality and novel.* In this sense creativity begins with high order intelligence in order to produce products or ideas that are high in quality, but creative people go beyond what can be produced by intelligence alone to produce something novel. The creative product may or may not be considered valuable or of high quality by contemporary society, since those in positions of power are often not thrilled to see their work challenged or the assumptions on which their work is based questioned.

It is important to understand, however, that intelligence is a prerequisite for creativity because creative people not only produce ideas of high quality, they also discriminate among all the ideas they produce to choose the best ones to promote. They learn in one sense to redefine the problem and apply their new and best thinking to its solution.

A look at the extraordinary material comfort and constantly improving technological wizardry achieved in the past century gives unequivocal proof of the vast numbers of intelligent and creative people alive in our world at this time. At the same time, however, can we be confident that "goodness" will prevail?

Wisdom Transcends Both Intelligence and Creativity

Both intelligence and creativity working together are the necessary prerequisites for wisdom. Writing in the April 2001 issue of *The American Psychologist*, Dr. Robert Sternberg says "Wisdom represents a synthesis of intelligence and creativity." Wise individuals balance the need for change (creativity) and the need for continuity and stability (intelligence). Sternberg says they are the most effective and sought after in positions of leadership. Indeed, they are the vanguard of humanity's evolving consciousness.

Life evolves to survive. Living organisms, including humans, continue to evolve in response to changing conditions. An interesting example of this was reported recently in *The Vancouver Sun*. Apparently a small mosquito living in eastern North America is responding to global climate change by depositing its eggs later and later in the season, thus giving its offspring the best chance for success in a longer warmer season. The genes of this new mutation were strongly represented in the population and, according to the scientist's theory, would soon take over the species. This is an example in microcosm of the way living species survive and even flourish in changing conditions.

It is clear that humans continue to evolve in our technological world environment towards greater intellectual complexity that produces a consciousness adaptive to our more complex times. Survival as a species needs to turn that complexity towards life-enhancing solutions. Thus, it is not surprising to see huge numbers of intelligent and creative people learning to adapt in more balanced and wiser ways to the threats against the environment and against their health and well-being. Responses also show strong impulses to live together more harmoniously in communities that nurture, respect and support life. The genes and the consciousness of this cohort will prevail against those who use their intelligence and creative talent to destroy others.

This is not to say that evolutionary or biological principles, or indeed God, will look after everything. We must strive wisely and with good intention to understand how our environment has changed since September 11 in order to address both the ongoing threat of terrorism and the imbalance in world conditions that provide fertile grounds to sustain the root causes of terrorism.

Examining the Terrorist Psyche

There is a great temptation in looking at the terrible destruction of the World Trade Towers to see this as the work of senseless, mindless, insane people. According to Philip Zimbardo in his article "Opposing Terrorism by Understanding the Human Capacity for Evil," in the *Monitor of Psychology,* November 2001, this would be wrong for two reasons: 1) the perpetrators acted with clearly defined purposes; and 2) they had a high level of reasoned intellect behind their deeds.

Thus, in terms of our definitions above they were highly intelligent and used a novel or creative approach to perpetrate their evil. Therefore, in order to prevent their future success we need to actively and directly address the human conditions that allow thousands of people to support and indeed cheer on the destruction of other human beings. Knowing how such kinds of evil almost destroyed all of civilization in the 20th century, however, we do not have the luxury of demanding peace at any price as many, though not all, well-meaning peace movements are doing.

Nor can we allow ourselves simply to point to easily made connections between the poverty in the world and the disparities between rich and poor countries as the cause of the terrorism. Those who committed these atrocities were not poor themselves and are likely using these conditions and even manipulating and maintaining them for their own purposes.

To address the current battle against terrorists who would use their intelligence and creativity to perpetrate evil, we must use our own power and the result of our technological intellect and creativity to destroy their bases of power. To do otherwise would be to surrender to the fear their acts and intentions engender and to leave the legacy we hand on to our descendants, and indeed their survival, under continuous threat of future destruction.

Wisdom Will Prevail

Never before in history has the challenge for an evolved consciousness been greater. Never has the struggle for good over evil been more complex. To succeed we must allow the complexity to stand and engage both in addressing creative evil and in redressing the root causes that would allow it to flourish in the future.

Given the millions of people now alive on the planet capable of this complex and wisdom-based response, and given that many of them are in positions of leadership at every level, I am confident that the response that intends to support life enhancement will win over those whose creative intent is bent on destruction. In the end, such consciousness will invite its own destruction.

The genetic pool of people in every nation bent on supporting life strengthens the adaptive, creative and wise response. It is this cohort who will ultimately prevail and win the war. In the future their influence and their genes will survive in every community where the struggle takes place.

In our present moment of urgent challenging conditions no human quality is more important than wisdom—a wisdom deeply embedded in our human psyche that is acutely intelligent, sharply focused on developing creative solutions and tenderly compassionate towards all life. At the same time, this wisdom needs to be tempered with great courage to overcome the current *soldiers of terror*, and even more important to continue in sustained and creative endeavour to win the more subtle battles for justice and equity that follow.

In every act of sustaining good, from family to nation, each of us has the great opportunity to contribute. I am confident about our future, because I know there are tens of millions already engaged in acts of inspiring human nobility and goodness. Post September 11 many more have been roused to join the fight. Against this army no evil force has a chance, regardless of what divine source they invoke to explain their dastardly actions.

I am thus inspired to be among the generations now alive who have the opportunity to secure for our descendants a world in which wisdom prevails.

November, 2001

The Evolution of Consciousness:

Scientific Evidence for Win-Win as the Basic Principle Underlying Life

Early in 1961 the electric words embedded in the inaugural address of President John Fitzgerald Kennedy lit up the minds of a generation of global citizens in formation. "Ask not," he said, "what your country can do for you, but what *you* can do for your country." It was for our generation who were used to reaping the rewards of a the post-war economy in North America, a new, exciting and different question, although we knew the ancient and universal injunction of all the religions of history: "How can I serve the common good?"

At the same time, the consciousness of the overwhelming majority of my generation was filled with mind-numbing trivial questions like, "What shall I wear to the party tonight? What should I cook for dinner? What film should we see, etc.?" Those of us still studying at schools and universities also had our consciousness stuffed with the often trivial details of the content of our courses, focused on memorizing enough to get the best possible grades to earn our diplomas so to advance our own careers.

Bent on acquiring the "stuff" of the good life—a home, a spouse, a car, a holiday—we did not address the pivotal question: "How might we use our gifts and talents to serve the world?"

By the 1960s human consciousness was shifting gears. Out of the horrors of two world wars and the holocaust, phoenix-like the

United Nations had emerged to set a new standard for the common good. Central to this drive was the Universal Declaration of Human Rights, championed by Eleanor Roosevelt and passed into human law and consciousness with 48 founding countries voting in favour and eight abstaining. It declared that human rights were *universal* and not subject to the whims of any state. They are implicit to human life, and while these rights are imperfectly enjoyed in most of the countries voting in favour, and indeed denied in others (the abstaining countries included the USSR, Soviet block countries of Eastern Europe, South Africa and Saudi Arabia) they nevertheless reflected a high standard of world justice. Transgressing against them is now universally condemned by democratic countries and materially expressed in our time by such global institutions as the World Court of Justice at The Hague.

Not many years after President Kennedy made his inaugural remarks, youthful protesters were taking to the streets and campuses of the world's cities, protesting the Vietnam War and dispersing thousands of draft dodgers from their homes and native land. As the decades went on, the feminine voice began to speak out loud to demand and eventually achieve some space at board room tables in the highest halls of power in many countries. Leaders like Martin Luther King Jr. and Nelson Mandela inspired greater opportunity for blacks in America and the end of apartheid in South Africa, just as Mahatma Gandhi had gained freedom from colonial oppression in the Indian subcontinent decades earlier.

In millions of small and hard fought battles of conscience, the consciousness of the world moved towards higher ground, and the common idea of goodness is still evolving today, inch by unforgiving inch.

Two Examples of Progress

Two current examples will suffice to provide evidence of the tens of thousands of other events, which from the perspective of the 1950s and 60s expressed viewpoints that seem impossible.

In June 2002 a conference on "Character and Community" was held in the United States White House in Washington D.C. Hosted by First Lady Laura Bush and including such speakers as President George W. Bush and Secretary of State Colin Powell, it featured prominent psychologists' research on fostering children's ethical and moral development.

The First Lady opened the conference by extending education's three Rs with a fourth essential, "Responsibility." Secretary of Education, Rod Paige PhD, and the President himself explained how educators can teach the fourth R as well as fairness, sharing, trust, tolerance, respect and caring. Secretary Powell, referring to his own childhood in a South Bronx neighbourhood that looked after children as a community and modeled solid values, spoke to the real learning of good character, which is organized in the minds and hearts of children by watching adults model values of goodness.

Three things are significant about this event. First, the promise expressed by Colin Powell of the government's interest in "not only teaching students to do the right thing when no one is looking, but in encouraging adults to model doing the right thing when there is no reward." Second, that these ideas are put into public consciousness on the initiative of a First Lady (harkening back to President Kennedy's remarks), following in the footsteps of another former First Lady, Eleanor Roosevelt, and yet another, Hilary Clinton. Last, it is a *black* Secretary of State who grew up in a poor neigbourhood in America, who puts the ideas forward in words so elegant and poignant that they resonate with authenticity.

The second event so improbable in the 50s and 60s took place in January 2002 in Assisi, Italy, called "In the Name of Peace: the Assisi Decalogue." It was the largest meeting in history of the world's religious leaders. Participants at the Congress included Pope John Paul II and Bartholomew I, spiritual leaders of the Roman Catholic Christian Church and the Orthodox Christian Church respectively; Jewish Rabbis including some from Israel; 30 Muslim Imams from Iran, Iraq, Saudi Arabia, Egypt and Pakistan; Protestant Christian Ministers representing Baptists, Lutherans, Anglicans, Methodists, Presbyterians, Mennonites and Quakers; Buddhists; monks and gurus representing Hindus, Sikhs, Zoroastrians and Native African religions; as well as representatives from the World Council of Churches.

This assembly unanimously agreed in the following statement to **"Condemn every recourse to violence and war in the name of God or religion. . .** No religious goal can possibly justify the use of violence by man against man."

They issued a 10-commitment statement they called the Assisi Decalogue for Peace. In March the Pope sent a copy to Heads of State in the world.

The Assisi Decalogue begins: **"We commit ourselves to proclaiming our firm conviction that violence and terrorism are incompatible with the authentic spirit of religion..."**

The Assisi Decalogue continues by committing the religious leaders:

- to educate people to mutual respect and esteem

- to foster the culture of dialogue

- to forgive one another for past errors or prejudices

- to take the side of the poor and helpless

- to speak out for those who have no voice

- to urge leaders of nations to make every effort to create and consolidate a world of solidarity and peace based upon justice

Again, amazingly the world's religious leaders sat together to raise a common voice for a culture of peace, for a world based on human justice, and in support of "goodness" and against the perpetuation of evil and tyranny against humankind.

It is remarkable to know about these *under-reported* and critically important events, while the world media focus their reports on the terrorist acts, suicide bombers, the calls for holy wars of terrible and terrifying destruction, and calls for the responses of war against the "axis of evil," against those harbouring the intent to use weapons of mass destruction.

It is also remarkable to know about these events in the face of the reported conspiracy theories and the thousands of other acts against justice and against the support of a sustainable environment that come through the Internet and alternative media voices. This brings us to the conclusion that at least both kinds of events—the good and the evil—are occurring in the enormous complexity of the six billion of our species now living in the countries, cities, villages and communities of this planet.

Overarching Questions for Humanity

In the face of the world's conflict and complexity it behooves us to ask the overarching question about the future of the current cohort of humanity: Who will ultimately win and what does science, the most important tool and way of knowing of our time, have to say about this question—and about other questions of profound importance to the future of humanity:

What is the meaning of our presence here on this planet at this time? Why are we here?

Can human lives have noble purpose with or without accepting one of the various beliefs in a divine creator?

Where are we going? What is the future of a species with such a terrible history of war, murder and destruction?

These questions have no short or simple answers. However, some new thinking is coming from an emerging and to this point marginal corner of my own discipline of psychology. It is not being expressed, however, by young inexperienced and marginal thinkers in the field. Rather, the voices of this new area of psychology come from the elders and most prominent and respected in the field.

This thinking is coming from minds after three or more decades of excellent scientific work, central to the discipline and taking place in America's most revered universities.

It responds urgently to the need for balance in a field focused on mental illness and the psychometric measure of difficulties with learning and thinking. It turns the focus to the normal human condition, away from sadness and depression to happiness and the expression of strengths, virtues, giftedness and talent. It supplements what we know about madness to look at sanity and its potential contribution to the human future.

Positive Psychology

This new field called Positive Psychology by one of its founding elders, Martin Seligman PhD, President of the American Psychological Association for the year 2000, is described in his recently published (2002) book *Authentic Happiness.*

Positive psychology has three pillars:

1. The study of positive emotion.

2. The study of positive traits, strengths and virtues.

3. The study of positive institutions such as democracy, strong families and free enquiry that support all of the above.

In his book, Seligman reports on an event of note, much smaller in some ways but no less significant to the human future than the two reported above. This event was hosted in the Bahamas by Sir John Templeton, the billionaire founder of the Templeton Fund, whose Foundation gives away millions of dollars a year to support the unconventional scholarship that sits in the unfashionable borderland between Science and Religion.

The meeting was a conclave of 10 scientists, philosophers and theologians. Templeton, then 87 years old, is no slouch in the life of the mind. He was first in his class at Yale, a Rhodes Scholar, a voracious reader and a prolific author.

He opened the meeting with some central questions:

1. Can human lives have a noble purpose?

2. Can our lives have a meaning that transcends the meaning we merely create for ourselves?

3. Has natural selection set us on this very path of noble purpose and goodness?

The gathering included people with previous records as great thinkers both from the theological and secular sides of the question. Among them was Robert Wright, author of *The Moral Animal*, in which he argues that human morality has profound evolutionary underpinnings. At this meeting Wright suggested that the secret of life is not DNA, but another discovery made at the same time as Watson and Crick's discovery of DNA. It was put forward by John von Neumann and Oskar Morgenstern in their thesis that *"the nonzero-sum game or the win-win game is the basic principle underlying life."*

According to this thesis, the superior reproductive success favours win-win games. They promote more complexity and complex intelligence, which is the ultimate success of natural selection, especially when compared to the win-loss or zero-sum game of competition.

Further, and indeed more important for this discussion, it is not only biological change that has this direction, but human history itself. The more positive-sum games in a culture, the more likely it is to succeed and flourish.

While the reader must now forgive the oversimplification of the above most profound and complex statements, they do lead for the purposes of this discussion to considering the central question of this essay: *What about the future of humankind?*

Reaching the Bifurcation Point

Progress in nature does not usually happen in small, incremental steps alone. Instead, there is a build-up of events over time, which leads to a bifurcation point and a breakthrough to the next level of evolutionary success.

Further, we now know that in our time the bifurcation must lead to a new and evolved consciousness. The world is under enormous pressure to change. Indeed, our very survival depends on it, as all around us old thinking that has led in the past, especially the recent past, to war, death and destruction of both the cultural and natural world continues to play the zero-sum, win-lose games.

Warnings and the evidence of the results of this thinking abound. Vaclav Havel, President of the Czech Republic, articulates this with the following prophetic cry: "Without a global revolution in the sphere of human consciousness, nothing will change for the better. . . and the catastrophe towards which the world is headed—the ecological, social, demographic or general breakdown of civilization—will be unavoidable."

Ervin Laszlo in his book *Macroshift* (2001) speaks to this point. The breakdown of civilization is not unavoidable. Our consciousness can be evolved. If each of us would evolve his or her consciousness, this "Holos-consciousness" would swell into a mighty tide that could change the world.

The answer from science is clear and unequivocal. Natural selection favours as winners those who play the win-win game. Millions of win-win games are taking place worldwide. Even the media focus on win-lose cannot hide the fact that world consciousness and conscience is getting better and better.

The same Internet that circulates the bad stories also reports the struggles for goodness. It is important to note that just because they are not reported in the mainstream media does not mean they are not taking place. Eventually the balance will tip and breakthroughs will happen everywhere.

While the oil fires burn, the world will eventually adopt a new range of non-polluting power sources. While the wars rage on, the urge for peace will eventually overcome and the peace dividend will provide through improved science, technology, business opportunity and moral imperative, an end to the kind of hunger and poverty we are now witnessing. New forms of representative government based on the democracies of today will take over the governance of the world. The shift from competition to alliance now endorsed by multilevel trade treaties and the European Union will become the norm.

The journey ahead is neither short or without danger, but the forces for goodness are gathering. We are hundreds of millions strong, and the future is pregnant with our progeny. May the year 2003 bring us closer to their birth!

December, 2002

Towards a New Spirituality:

The Hope for the Future

In our family a new child was born this week. For me this miracle of life renewing itself brings strong focus on the legacy our generation will leave to those now small and vulnerable human beings who eventually take our place in the wondrous story and web of life.

The world into which they come looks full of violence and the despair that such acts bring to ordinary people. The children born post September 11, 2001 inherit in their birth year a world traumatized not only by the event itself, but also by the effect of its televised images of horror burned into our consciousness. No wonder we are preoccupied by security

How is it then, infused with these images myself, with psyche bruised by them and the responses that follow, that I am nevertheless enormously hopeful for the children in my family and the world? It is because we are forced to see the bigger picture and to engage in creating the future different and better than the past. I look to my own legacies and the victories during my lifetime for a more civil and just society. However bad the circumstances of the present moment arc cithcr for pcacc or the planet, I look deeper than current events as reported by the media, deeper than known facts such as 9/11, deeper than written history, to the very nature of our species itself, to the emergence of the consciousness we experience in ourselves that is the legacy of 10,000 generations

History tells the stories of military victories because the heroic giants of the past, the "Greats," were the conquerors, celebrated for their conquests, regardless of the means, the cruelty, the unconcern for the victims. Significantly, however, our genes tell a different history, since the six billion of us now on the planet have as much of the vanquished as the victors in us. Indeed, some of the great leaders and players on the world stage had grandparents who were slaves and impoverished refugees. One might then ask, how did this come about, and what, therefore, can we reliably predict for the future of this small boy born in the last week of January 2002.

New Evidence from Science

Late 20th century science is revealing a startling picture of how and why our species has survived in spite of a history of continuous warfare, blood-lust, power mongering and fierce competition of every kind. Further, this understanding is pointing the way to how we can create a more secure, quality future for our descendants that includes peaceful co-existence and nurturance in our relationships, our families, our communities and our nations.

While this whole cultural transformation will probably take several generations to mature, each individual who understands the concepts on which it is built and participates can benefit. As the world moves to embrace this new thinking with greater knowledge and intention, each generation will benefit more.

While the underlying story of our survival is still largely unknown, new pieces are rapidly emerging as the puzzle of our DNA is unraveled. We are being revealed as an integrated organism, a living system in which every part from the tiniest particle of us to the consciousness we experience as mind is one whole. Moreover, just as our cells are part of us, we are part of a living planet, which in turn is part of the solar system and the galaxies and, indeed, the whole universe—all are parts of the same whole too vast for our imaginations to understand.

Nor are life, birth, death and the immaterial spirit that infuses each of us clearly understood. These new uncertainties call for a different kind of spirituality, just as surely as the understanding that the Earth is not flat, and is not the centre of the universe, called for a rethinking of who and what we are. Spirituality, which was once restricted to the relationship between a supernatural divine power and us, now needs to include a sacred respect for the "whole," the living planet and all its life, especially human life. It is no longer wise to speak from positions of certainty about spiritual truth, regardless from what ancient and sacred source, since the very assumptions of who we are change continuously. It would be more reasonable and sensible to see these traditions as a profoundly important but evolving story, based on the known of their generations. From that position we can look to some things we do not know for new answers and indeed new and deep questions.

Survival of the Good

We know that everywhere in the living families that fill the biosphere that mothers and fathers have nurtured, protected and provided for their young. We also know that in all of life, our species included, these life enhancing actions generate electrochemical responses that benefit our immune system, support health and wellness, and boost the powerful dynamic physical and mental energy that powers our life and work. Indeed, thousands of scientific studies reliably indicate that the nurturing and positive activities we experience as love, caring and compassion produce more fighter "T" cells, more NK cells, macrophages, IGA, etc. that support our immune system's ability to recover. By these acts we heal, live longer, feel better, and produce and nurture more healthy young. These human qualities, regardless of culture, have been promoted and defended by women whose responsibility for bearing and nurturing life has been primary to the continuation of our species.

The spiritual ideas of the future will need to include the fact that we are one whole organism on a living planet in a living universe whose life depends on nurture, collaboration and service to thrive. It will need to reject any cultural belief that acts against this knowing. The new spirituality will not tolerate any act against life from any source.

At the centre of this new spirituality is a deep abiding respect for women, for men, for children, and for people of every age, each of whom carries the whole legacy of a vast and wondrous system. Indeed, as knowledge progresses we become aware that we understand only as much of this whole wonder as an ant understands its anthill. Still, knowing the tiniest bit of information we must act to protect the discoveries that lie in the future, since as surely as we know the miracle of a child's birth, we know how awesome and astounding these revelations will be.

In the meantime we must act with sustained courage and perseverance against those who act against life, knowing that the history of the "goodness" of our species is at least as long as the stories of our wars, our cruelty and our ferocity. These last months since September 11 have shown the potential for our nobility as a species. In the 21st century, as awful as its first year has been, we have also seen some wonderful and even surprising acts of new examples of an emerging global spiritual understanding: acts that demonstrate our disgust at the treatment of women in Afghanistan and insist on their presence in the new governance of that country; acts against terrorism, the ultimate "disrespecter" of life; and acts that save human lives in war-torn and volcano-ravaged communities.

The benefits of aggression and cruelty are short term in the human history of 10,000 generations. Our DNA reveals that the benefits of compassion and nurture are long term. In the microcosm of an individual life, engaging in relationships that support and foster goodness pays off in great dividends over that lifetime.

The exciting story for a child born this week is how many hundreds of millions know and practice this, regardless of what language they speak or what culture or religion they practice. Never before in the history of our species have we been so many.

Cause for Hope

Our task, therefore, is to connect in this web of life and to tell and write the stories of this new spirituality into every language and culture. As we have become more cognitively intelligent and productive during the last marvel of a century for progress in science, technology and human health and comfort, so the task of the next century is for us to become wiser, more thoughtful, more honest, more trustworthy, life embracing and spiritually intelligent. With such a task ahead, and the legacy of progress we've already inherited, it is no wonder I am hopeful for my grandson born this week.

February, 2002

Evolving Our Consciousness
With Intention

We are a chauvinistic species. We assume that *our time* is *"the time."*
We suspect that just ahead is "white water" and beyond that may be
a "Niagara-like falls." We arrogantly assume that there has never
before been a species or civilization like ours because we don't *know*
about them. This is the same kind of thinking as existed in the days
of Christopher Columbus. America did not exist because Europeans
did not know about it. In reality it was there all the time, waiting to
be discovered. We have good reason to believe that the evidence of
past civilizations as accomplished as ours in many respects is there
waiting to be discovered. The reason that they disappeared without
a trace is that they did not evolve their consciousness to deal with
the white water and Niagara-like falls of their time. Can we be more
successful by evolving our consciousness on purpose?

To do this we will have to pay attention to something our
palaeontologists and anthropologists have not been considering
in their study of the evolution of life on the planet. This is the
idea that the *content of consciousness* is the determining factor
that creates the nature of reality in every society. We come to
this idea from contemporary understanding of consciousness as a
living, electrochemical energy moving in a continuous loop system,
mediated by two non-local organs, the brain and the heart. Sending
their messages via blood and neurotransmitters, they signal the
intricately complex network of receptors lodged in every cell. This

activates all the body systems, including the nervous and immune system, to carry on the business of life. From this we know that what we are thinking, the content of consciousness, affects ourselves, but goes further, beyond the skin, to affect all our human relationships and potentially even the living systems of animals and plants we either care for or abuse.

Our reductionist science has not been particularly helpful to us in understanding ourselves as a whole. If we did pay attention, we would see that we function as a collaborative-cooperative, self-nurturing, self-healing system. To the degree that our consciousness is fueled by positive, life-enhancing content, its systems generally function well. One part of our biological system cannot wage war on another without serious penalty to the whole. The same is true in ecosystems. Thus, as the content of human consciousness moves towards collaboration, cooperation, nurturing and service, it moves in harmony with the natural laws of the universe.

Great leaders from the past and the illumined minds who founded the great spiritual traditions, all understood this principle of nature. Yet the dominant history of our species shows that the content of consciousness that has held sway for most of the time has been rooted in thinking that was competitive, violent and destructive. Leaders in the past who leaned towards nurturance were alone or isolated or just too few in number to make a real difference. Today we are at the same point. But there are nevertheless many whose consciousness contains the positive effect of life-enhancing nurturance; and the "netways," electronic highways between minds, are open, though perhaps congested. Through print and electronic and personal contact, minds can meet and embrace, producing a "love dividend," which may be invested in the cause of survival, transformation and evolution of ourselves and our descendants. The negative forces of destruction may persist all around us, but if we know the stakes, we can choose to evolve on purpose by learning to live in harmony with the natural laws of collaboration, nurturance and service.

We have the further advantage in that each living consciousness is a centre that is at the same time a part of the whole. Each of us, at the centre of our own network of relationships, may choose to act in an evolved, life-enhancing way. If there is to be a chance for the future, it will be in the acts of millions of such evolved persons acting to send the ripple of service into their own networks. Most importantly, the spark, the flame, the added power that occurs in the synchrony of such mind embraces, could transform the world. It is my passionate and fervent hope that it will.

November, 1994

The Feminine
Perspective

Wherever societies have respected our humanity and allowed a voice to women as well as men, those communities have flourished. It is the one principle across cultures that stands out in history as a universal good.

The nurturing phenomenon, whether personally experienced or culturally generated, makes women think differently from men about life and its meaning. As women increasingly sit in board rooms of corporations or government, as they experience high office and take charge of business, they bring this underlying perspective to the table, whether they recognize it or not. Schooled in the very essence of life's meaning, they bring a different perspective to decision making, which provides important lessons to those interested in ethical leadership.

Women understand that survival is dependent on urgent action on a daily basis in tiny steps. They know that health is best managed by prevention--like proper food, sleep and nutrition--and they continually work from crisis to crisis as the vagaries of infection, injury and life's fortunes impact their family. From this they learn to get to the heart of it, to create a day from rising to sleeping that has some good in it. They do not delay or hold back the needed comfort.

Ethical Leadership:

The Applied Wisdom of the Feminine Perspective

Something happens inside a woman's consciousness when she gives birth to a child that forever changes the adolescent in her. She becomes the practical nurturer with every cell of her being. Talking about doing the right thing by the child is not enough. "Right action" must take place in response to an urgent agenda that is not her own. The baby must be fed, changed, comforted, and the nest made conducive to safety and growth twenty-four hours a day. She becomes an adult whose goodness is directed to ensuring the next generation prospers.

As the child grows, the mother becomes by necessity educator and mentor. Through the quality of her nurturing the next generation flourishes or fades, blooms or wanes. (I have left the father's role out of the discussion for the moment and will come back to it.) No one has called this activity leadership. Indeed it is this very preoccupation with children's early nurturing that has forced women into second class citizenship as leaders and champions. Yet every known tradition values this "right action" at the heart of its moral code, and finds some way to protect this process as the price of the tribe's or society's survival.

Looking across to the natural world, the same phenomenon of the female as nurturer is central to most species' survival. With our species it is more pronounced, because the human child is born helpless and requires several years of careful nurturing for its powerful brain to develop to full potential.

Lessons for Leadership

The nurturing phenomenon, whether personally experienced or culturally generated, makes women think differently from men about life and its meaning. As women increasingly sit in board rooms of corporations or government, as they experience high office and take charge of business, they bring this underlying perspective to the table, whether they recognize it or not. Schooled in the very essence of life's meaning, they bring a different perspective to decision making, which provides important lessons to those interested in ethical leadership.

The first lesson is that the process of life is essentially democratic. All mothers do this nurturing. The act transcends every barrier of language, race and class. It is the great equalizer. Thus women in general are readier to ascribe skill across the strata of the community, and do not assume that competence is dependent on rank or birth.

Secondly, women understand that survival is dependent on urgent action on a daily basis in tiny steps. They know that health is best managed by prevention—like proper food, sleep and nutrition—and they continually work from crisis to crisis as the vagaries of infection, injury and life's fortunes impact their family. From this they learn to get to the heart of it, to create a day from rising to sleeping that has some good in it. They do not delay or hold back the needed comfort.

The third lesson we can learn from the mother's perspective is to be continuously amazed and astounded by the child's intelligence and good sense that engenders both awe and respect for human life. This is translated by mothers into what they understand to be love and loving acts. It is this phenomenon which brings us to the very heart of the lessons to be learned from the female perspective on life.

We have been enjoined by the creators of our traditions, mostly masculine, to "love one another" without truly understanding what the word "love" means. The word has been robbed of any specific meaning by its widespread application to all kinds of feelings. Spiritual traditions use it. New Age thinking is awash in its use.

Our culture uses it to sell every aspect of material life by promising it as reward for buying every product our imagination can conjure up. By such widespread use, no one dares speak against it, but few really know what it means to them.

However, mothers, whether they can give language to it or not, truly know that at the very basis of its meaning, love is the feeling of awe and respect for the loved one and indeed for all human life. That feeling is also directed at their mothers and sisters and themselves for having produced it. Somehow, because our society has devalued this phenomenon, the self esteem and respect and awe that is at the very source of life's survival has been distorted. Even so, women still bring this value to the table, often in spite of themselves.

What Does This Mean for Ethical Leadership?

When one strips away all the words, all the cultural overtrappings of every society, the value of awe and respect for life is at the very source of every positive emotion. Doing no harm to life, and nurturing it to the next seven generations has created the fundamental creed in every tradition. Wherever these values are distorted by the culture, humanity suffers. Fundamental to all this is the question that goes back one step further to the origin of everything: *How did all this incredible life and the planet needed for its sustenance come to be?*

The mystery generated by this wondering, despite current scientific explanations, goes to the core of our spirituality and begs the greater question: *Do we have the right to destroy what has been so divinely created?*

Thus, it is the respect and awe for life which is the basis of feminine consciousness, and life's task for the vast majority of us, is to empower the growth of that life to independent adulthood. What if we were to bring these feelings out into the open? What if we included them in the bottom line? What if we truly made them part of our decisions?

How then could we wage war, harm one another in business, and destroy the air, water and land along with the flora and fauna that sustain us?

These are not unworldly or idealistic questions. They are the most practical issues at the very base of reality. Of course a perfect response is not always possible, just as a child's need cannot always be fully met. We do the best we can, but we never knowingly go against the basic code, and we always keep the child's well-being in continuous consideration.

Now what about men? How do they figure in this equation? In this case people of my generation have something to learn from the young generation of men now becoming fathers. I observe my son and sons-in-law and those of my friends participating in active and important ways in every aspect of parenting, from the birth itself to the care and nurturing of the children. This is not about a new cultural phenomenon, but rather about masculine strength, which expresses the best of itself in its most noble form when it acts with gentleness in caring for and providing safe harbour to mother and child.

The ingredients that comprise this great soup of nurturing contain all the positive human values. Here we find the source of self-worth, of trust and trustworthiness, of integrity and authenticity. We need look no deeper than this common foundation of the world's cultures for an ethical transformation of an emerging global community as we come to the turn of the millennium. As we look at the essence of all communities, we shall find that their survival over time was dependent on the respect and awe for life of their members. Now, as global citizens of a global community, we must do no less on this broadest of all possible fronts.

This is the foundation on which we can build our new codes of life and law and business. On this life-giving principle we should build every new treaty. Considering this should be the basis of every new project. Indeed, if we finally did this, we could at last be proud of how we are handling the great heritage of life entrusted to us, and with equal pride hand it over to the generations that follow

December, 1997

A New Balance:

Giving Attention to the Feminine Voice

The material world pulses with the rhythm of a universe connected in a manner so complex and intricate and at a level so small that the microscope needed to see it has not yet been invented. The science through which we understand reality is at the cusp of such a transformation of knowing that all of our previous experience with such moments of change has not prepared the way. A trillion trillion threads at the quantum level are weaving themselves into new patterns of life, learning continuously how to be better adapted to the future ahead.

Decades away from this moment the pattern and the fabric of life will be so different we would not recognize it from our present vantage point. Like the growth of a child in our family, we cannot see the pattern changing because our daily observations are not able to detect the minute changes taking place in front of us, simple act by simple act, incident by incident.

Life adapts in order to continue. Great threats to our survival as a species have affected all life in the century just past. We saw them writ large on September 11, 2001 as the consciousness driven by hatred and bent on destruction had its way. While others might focus on the damaging effects of human activity on the environment and on the biosphere, I will raise my voice here to focus more deeply on what I see as the ultimate causal factors of the dangers of our time.

Fear and Attachment

Two primordial emotions govern all life: fear and attachment. To the degree that fear governs society we have seen war and suffering playing out the human drama of the last 10,000 years. The reason is that the way to overcome fear is to take control: to be bigger, stronger, faster, more cruel, more punishing and thus win the moment for yourself, your tribe, your nation. At the deepest levels of the consciousness that connects us, the pain and suffering along with the building of our current civilizations have been spurred by this fear.

But yet, if the only emotion receiving expression were fear, we would not have survived. Pulsing with the life force, and more powerful than fear, is the binding power of attachment that begins when a mother cares for her young. Through the emotion of this attachment we learn a different truth than that of fear, and through this learning we create and nurture our common future.

It is the force of attachment that allows us to evolve our intelligence. While today's reality seems overcome by fear, there are a million trends that cumulatively can bring us to a bifurcation point where the balance tips away from fear towards attachment and nurture. The message then is to use our intelligence to view life and reality with the lens that searches out, reveals and highlights acts of goodness. These are the experiences that enhance life and give us the wisdom to understand the destructiveness of fear and to see fear mongering for what it is.

Raising the Voices of Women

Because the stakes are now so high and because the danger of the degradation of all life is so real, the importance of speaking out becomes essential for a new way of living together on this fragile planet. Feminine intelligence, genetically programmed for nurture and attachment, now needs to prevail, not by seeking to overcome but rather to redress the balance and bring the masculine intelligence to also see its nurturing side.

Can you imagine an Afghanistan where women are equally respected and as powerful as men? How different would it be from the country of today where the harboring of terror and the perpetration of fear have wreaked their devastation. Can you imagine a future for Afghanistan where mothers and daughters, educated along with fathers and sons, take an equal place in parliament and in the institutions and places of business and commerce and in the very life of the country?

Can you imagine an America, a Britain or a Russia where the mothers have equal voice?

Riane Eisler in her book, *The Chalice and the Blade*, tells of a time in history when the feminine voice was honoured and heard. In her book, *The Power of Partnership*, she provides hundreds of examples of how the reality of true partnering between men and women enhance every aspect of business and industry. In *Tomorrow's Children* she proposes that caring for life for the self, for others and for our Mother Earth should be a thread running through the educational curriculum from preschool to graduate school. It should be an integral part of every child's education. Can you imagine the communities of citizens who were educated in this way?

We need to foster the conditions that encourage caring relationships, and we can do this by building cultures worldwide that value the voices of women as equal partners.

Bringing Dignity to Global Life

We should examine how we are supporting without question through aid, trade and tourism countries that are denigrating half of their population through suppression. No wonder these societies are in a perpetual state of rage, anger and fear that we see acted out on our television screens. Deprived of the dignity caring and nurture could create in *this* life even regardless of economic prosperity, they see themselves as better off dead so they can reap the reward of life after death. A people infused with such beliefs cannot possibly create the conditions that would make this life worth living.

There is a great need for a new global value system that honours the need of life, all life, for care, nurture and attachment. There is a great need for honesty with regard to the short-term gain that comes from agreeing to perpetuate lesser values in countries that are not prepared to come up to this standard.

Wherever societies have respected our humanity and allowed a voice to women as well as men, those communities have flourished. It is the one principle across cultures that stands out in history as a universal good.

Restoring the Balance

Today in the Western world a million trends are pushing in the direction of a new balance, a new human partnership. In institutions of higher learning classes of lawyers, doctors and scientists are now half filled with women. Boardrooms of institutions of big business are moving to include the feminine voice, and small businesses everywhere are benefiting from the energy and enterprise of women. Attention is now given to the wisdom and thoughtfulness of women elders. Wherever this is happening there is a benefit to the human commons.

Closer to Home

This week as I celebrated the birthdays of my two granddaughters I was moved to see how the simplest innocent act of a child exemplifies the important principles described at length above. My six-year old granddaughter, watching me enjoy her birthday cake beamed her satisfaction saying, "and I chose one without chocolate so you could eat it, too." She knows I have an allergy to chocolate. Her mother told me how she stayed up late the night before decorating each of the loot bags for her twelve little friends with specially created cartoons and individual objects they would personally enjoy.

As we observe our children grow, how utterly important it is in every family to support such acts of caring whatever form they take; for it is by these acts that we shall live and even thrive into the decades and centuries ahead.

May, 2002

Leadership

To engender trust a leader must be trustworthy. To promote justice, one must be just. To engage enthusiasm, be enthusiastic. In other words, a leader must model all the qualities and characteristics he or she expects of others. To coach, one must know how to play the game oneself. Indeed, such leadership demands that we never ask others to do something we are unwilling to do ourselves.

Leadership as the
New Millennium Begins

We are truly living in an unprecedented time, an age in which an evolved human consciousness is in the process of changing the world. Co-existing as one part of a whole spectrum of human consciousness, from the most primitive to the most advanced, this surge of new thinking raises compelling questions about the kind of leadership the world needs at the cusp of the millennium. In essence, the challenge is to link together the growing cohort of thinkers whose wise stewardship can lead this planet to a place where an evolved species of *homo sapiens sapiens* can flourish in an historic safe harbour.

To join this cohort requires credentials of a different kind from those that appear on walls as diplomas granted by institutions of higher learning still practicing 20th century thinking. The credentials of the new leaders will be evident through acts of courage, through modeling right action even in the face of risk, through dedicated loyalty, integrity and great enthusiasm for the group's *raison d'être*.

To become such a leader. one needs to focus on the journey itself, how the game of life and work is played, and not only on the destination or the bottom line. At the same time, such a leader keeps the end in mind, expects an outstanding outcome, uses rigorous rational thinking, and especially focuses on the big picture, even while mired in the daily blur of detail.

To be such a leader one needs to understand how to generate, nurture and sustain outstanding performance in oneself and others. The emphasis must be on the prime cause of achieving difficult goals. Such leaders need to know what strategies and safeguards are required to produce outstanding results with ordinary people.

Which leads us to investigate the power of relationships to create within individuals the ability to perform at such high levels, and within teams to achieve seemingly impossible goals.

The Power of Relationships

To understand the power of relationships, we need to consider what our current scientific knowledge of the nature of consciousness says about the very fabric of our humanity.

We are beginning to revise our understanding of who we are as human beings and what we are made of. We know now that we are not material entities with fixed physical limits like machines, but rather we are energy systems undergoing dynamic, continuous renewal. We are not a body, a mind and a spirit, but a whole living being in which all systems are interconnected and entirely governed by mind. Significantly, that mind is not only in the head, but in every cell of the body, so integrated and exquisitely tuned that a single thought produces a flood of neurochemical action that either engages or depresses action instantly. Even questions of health, and indeed life and death, can now be answered by our understanding of how the mind affects the immune system's response to its challenges.

Cloaked with this exquisite human organism, we are also attuned to each other, such that the whole of us responds with extraordinary sensitivity to each other, in both physical and mental ways, whether we intend this to happen or not.

Thus, it is in the relationships between us that the power of outstanding performance lies. The championship team, the outstanding business success, events of personal, national and international heroism or greatness, all are fully dependent on the elusive spirit of relationships within the team. The reason for this lies in the nature of who we are and what we need in order to function effectively.

Safe Harbour and Clarity of Purpose

All human beings need safe harbour for them to do their best work. To have this they must be able to trust the people close to them. Along with trust comes a sense of dignity, respect and encouragement, supported by a conviction that honesty, justice, fairness and integrity govern the actions of the group. Without this people enter the forum of daily activity with the need to protect themselves, to look after their own case, which detracts from whatever focus they need to do their work.

Once safe harbour is achieved, people need to be energized by clarity of purpose, a feeling that the job they are doing is important and that it is right that they do it. Indeed, they must be so convinced of its importance and rightness that they will risk courageously to achieve it. They must personally be part of the action. They need to have a role to play, to be counted on for their individual competent contribution. They need to know that the team is counting on them and expects them to do their best.

Related to this is the power of creativity. The creative impulse to invent new responses when old solutions are not producing the best result must be enthusiastically supported even in the face of potential temporary failure.

Which leads us then to ask how all this is related to leadership. How can a leader generate such spirit in others, and nurture and sustain it to respond effectively to the challenges of the new times?

Begin with Oneself

The answer emerges with starling simplicity—begin with oneself. To engender trust a leader must be trustworthy. To promote justice, one must be just. To engage enthusiasm, be enthusiastic. In other words, a leader must model all the qualities and characteristics he or she expects of others. To coach, one must know how to play the game oneself. Indeed, such leadership demands that we never ask others to do something we are unwilling to do ourselves.

Those who would develop leaders for a new time must be ready to walk their talk, to go first into risk, while at the same time being ready to double back and bring up the rear, if that is where the greater danger lies. Through all this action, the leader will pay constant attention to the relationships with each member of the team, providing new access when necessary, always ensuring that the relationships among the team members model the leader's relationship with them. This includes healthy competitiveness for place and promotion, so long as the overall safety of the unit is preserved by everyone accepting that responsibility.

Which leads us to rethink what we mean by a hero.

The New Hero

From antiquity and through history, the title and respect of hero has gone to the conqueror—to Alexander, to Caesar, to Napoleon, to Peter the Great. Mesmerized by their achievements, the world has thought less about the land they desecrated and the people they subjugated. Even in modern times wealth and power continue to be regarded as the criteria of greatness, regardless of the harm done to others in the pursuit of those ends.

However, as we move into the post-modern era, a new spirit is abroad that denies the acceptability of achieving greatness through doing harm to others. On the world stage, from the brutal leadership of the Serbs and Bosnians with their policies of ethnic cleansing, and the monstrous behaviour of Saddam Hussein in the Middle East and the butchers in Rwanda, to the silent willingness of Swiss banks to profit from Nazi atrocities--all this is being exposed, challenged and denounced by the free world and its media. Closer to home in our own country, acting without integrity, or lying and cheating to win either in politics or sport is being challenged on every front. Within the largest or smallest enterprise, from the Department of Defense and monolithic power utilities to the local corner store or small business contractor, trustworthiness and integrity are demanded by the client or consumer of goods and services.

So we live now in a world of transition and the resulting confusion. We are reluctant to give up the tarnished heroes of the past, while we expect something different from the heroes of the present, but still remain fascinated by the scoundrels who masquerade as leaders in real life and who leap out at us daily from the disturbed imaginations of those who craft the mainstream stories of television and film.

Which brings us to the question: How then shall we live?

Choosing the Way

The person who chooses to live with emotional health in such a world as described above, will find the way by joining the cohort of new leaders and new heroes who champion the cause of "right action" beginning with themselves. The reward for such leadership goes well beyond wealth, power or position. It comes from the opportunity to live a life of meaning, to make a difference, to leave the world better for the life you lived, to provide a better place for those who follow you.

Pushing your own potential to its limit allows you to transcend yourself as the energy system you know you surely are. If this is done in the direction of right action, you will live a healthy quality life. The relationships you model for others return to you to empower you in body-mind-spirit to produce the best of who you are.

Such rewards are priceless. Being on a life path that allows such traveling, is the ultimate and most sacred human journey.

January, 2001

Anti-Semitism

In response to each unspeakable act of evil we must raise ten million flags for good. No matter what benefit is promised, in democratic countries we must never vote for those whose policy or agenda is built on harming others. Especially in our ordinary everyday lives we must stand up and fight for decent action whether the wrong is perpetrated against us or anyone else. It is not good enough to say, "It doesn't involve us... Let them work it out... I'm okay... I'll just walk away from this." To act like this in small ways allows whole generations to adopt values which could lead to their collusion in some future time with those who would perpetrate crimes against individuals, nations and races.

"Why Do They Hate Us?"

A Response to the Legacies of Anger and Hatred
As the Future Weapons of Mass Destruction

Because it is such a privilege to share one's deeply held thoughts with an audience of thoughtful and wise colleagues around the world, I look forward to taking the time from the pressure of work-filled days and other obligations to write my contribution to *The Visioneer* newsletter. This time I admit to having procrastinated without just excuse, other than the difficulty of finding words to express the deep convictions and some misgivings now stirring in my mind.

These last months of UN debate around whether to go to war with Iraq, the invitations from America and Britain to join their coalition of the willing, the war itself, the aftermath, the revelations of the gruesome evil of Saddam Hussein's regime, and the current continuation of the terror in Israel in response to attempts to begin discussions about peace—all these have affected me profoundly. Nor do the new initiatives centred around the US Roadmap provide much confidence that peace will be the outcome of this very fragile and flawed process.

As awful as the deaths on all sides are, they seem a part of life as we know it in these last gruesome decades. What strikes me as newly revealed is the underlying personal anger, hatred and rage of hundreds of millions of people against America, the West and the Jews, and against the victories for tolerance, for justice, for women, for multiculturalism, and for the extension of the democratic process. Indeed, it is these very victories that have allowed me and the Canadians of my generation to succeed, to create a generation of educated, intelligent and secure children who are now parenting the next secure and fortunate generation.

Positive Psychology

The reason the anger is so distressing becomes clear unwittingly as I pursue my own agenda of creating my own work goals and hopes for the next decade of my working life. Searching within my own discipline of psychology for new knowledge that fits my thinking after 25 years of practice, I pursue with intense interest the emerging field of positive psychology.

Initiated and invigorated by the elders and eminent practitioners of American psychology, Martin E.P Seligman, Ray Fowler and Milhaly Csikszentmihalyi at a shared holiday in Mexico in January 1998, its purpose was to turn the field of psychology from the study of mental illness, disabilities and insanities to the study of human strength, virtue and mental health. They proposed to study human nobility, positive emotions, positive personal characteristics and positive institutions like democracy and the family. It is from this source that some considerations for solutions will emerge.

A Personal Experience with Hatred

A personal experience with hatred remains embedded in my psyche. More than 20 years ago in the early 1980s, I attended a meeting in Baden, Austria just outside Vienna. The hotel was supposedly one of those used as headquarters by the Nazis in World War II. My level of discomfort with this seemingly benign place was so huge that I chose to move to a hotel in downtown Vienna.

The Strasse lined with outside coffee houses and shops seemed cosmopolitan and sophisticated. I awoke on the morning of August 6 to the sound of goose-stepping soldiers. Outside my window crowds of people were parading on Hiroshima Day, shouting slogans and carrying placards with signs in the languages I understood— English, French and German—"Down with America", "Death to the

Jews", along with signs reflecting the supposed purpose of the day, such as "Never Again" and "Peace." I could not fathom how the Nazi symbols and peace marching fit together, but the volume, the frenzy, and what seemed then to a naïve and innocent Canadian, a kind of feigned anger, rose and fell in front of me. I ventured out for a few moments, but the pulse and hardness of the crowd so frightened me that I retreated and took the train to the Conference Centre, back to rational colleagues who played down my seriously frightened response.

I tell this old story because in the last few months, the parade, its frenzy and its hatred has played out again in front of my eyes, this time on television and magnified one thousand fold on the streets of various places in Europe and the Middle East. I needed to stop and examine again why these scenes so filled me with dread.

Authentic Happiness

Some answers came from a book by Marty Seligman called *Authentic Happiness*. In it Marty reports a dialogue with Robert Wright, author of the book *Non-Zero The Logic of Human Destiny* (based on the thesis that success in biology and life favours win-win [non-zero sum] relationships, rather than win-lose [zero sum].

Seligman wonders whether negative emotion evolved to help us in win-lose games. When we are in deadly competition, when it is eat or be eaten, when we are struggling to avoid loss and to repel trespass—when these are the conditions confronting us, then fear, anxiety, sadness and anger are our motivations and our guides. Further, it is well known that when embraced by the anonymity of crowds that expression of this negative emotion is magnified manyfold.

What then was causing the enormous anger that I felt surging on the street that long ago day in Vienna and that we witnessed on our TV screens these last few months, and where oh where will it take us?

Some Lessons from History Might Be of Use

A book called *The Anti-Semitic Moment* by Pierre Birnbaum reports on the 1897 riots in France following the Dreyfus affair.

Alfred Dreyfus, a Jewish captain wrongly convicted of treason, is defended by Emile Zola in an open letter to the President of the French Republic called, "J'accuse." In it he denounces the army leaders and proclaims Dreyfus innocent. Birnbaum, a professor of politics and philosophy at the Sorbonne, builds his viewpoint through a painstaking study of newspapers, pamphlets, journals, police records and speeches throughout France, writing as if he were an *embedded journalist* about the Anti-Semitic riots that follow. He describes the street demonstrators, the parades, the marches, the burned effigies, the vociferous and out of control mobs, their screams, their slogans, their rage to destroy Jewish shops and break down the doors of synagogues. He describes in detail from police reports one incredible scene that could have taken place on our TV screens this last month.

The protagonists were students from Paris University—law students and others from the schools of physics, dentistry and natural history. Three hundred of them assembled on the Place du Pantheon, danced around a bonfire, climbed through the windows of the closed law school, took the Rue Victor-Cousin, then Boulevard Saint-Michel. He reports on the cries of the rioters, "Down with the Jews", "Bring back the Inquisition", "France for the French", and so on.

In Germany at roughly the same time a new form of racism emerged based on spurious science proclaiming the superiority of the Aryan race and the ultimate corruption of the "Jewish race." Shortly afterwards Europe burst into race riots, politicians ran for office on anti-Semitic tickets, mobs spilled out into the streets attacking Jews and pillaging synagogues. In this period "The Patriots of the Elders of Zion" was written, a clumsy but immensely popular forgery of a supposed meeting of Jewish elders plotting to take over the world. In Austria violent anti-Semitic riots were led by the Mayor of Vienna, Karl Leuger, Hitler's inspiration. Russia exploded in a series of pogroms. The rest is known history.

Considering the 20th century outcomes only a decade or so following these events, one cannot help but wonder where the same kind of street violence magnified by the television play and replay of these events will lead in the 21st century. The danger is exacerbated when anger, hatred and revenge are taught to children in schools, written as gospel in their text books, preached venomously from the pulpits by their most revered elders, and popularized by the television screens so that it is the daily fare, not just of angry young men, but of every citizen.

Fergal Keane, a prominent BBC special correspondent, recognized for an award for outstanding commitment to journalistic integrity wrote, "Does the West understand how this Hatred War is altering the Arab world?" The war in Iraq was one war with two stories. On the day the war officially ended eight major newspapers in Cairo printed only two out of more than 100 war related photos of Iraqis interacting positively with coalition troops. For Arabs the faces of war were children with limbs blown off. Americans find it hard to believe that they would be so mercilessly attacked in the Arab press the day after jubilant Iraqis greeted the US led force in Baghdad.

And the warriors themselves on all sides are children, 18-25 year olds, who yesterday filled the halls of high school classrooms, returning to their communities hardened by war and by bearing witness to and even committing atrocities they could not even imagine months earlier.

Thus, with all this anger, this rage, this loss of innocence, how can we in protected Western countries create different legacies for our grandchildren, when the momentum, the march and the force of history seems to so overwhelmingly favour the display of negative emotion and the win-lose of the zero-sum game?

An Answer

Our chance lies in the very design of our species and that our destiny is to greater and greater complexity, which produces an enormous momentum towards win-win. As we create more knowledge, we accumulate greater power that carries with it the force for goodness of a kind never previously understood or expressed.

A small example is the story of how in the face of an upcoming war in Iraq, where an undernourished, water-deprived population struggled for existence, the World Health Organization, UNICEF and the Red Crescent combined their efforts to eliminate polio in Iraq. From February 23-28, 2003, fourteen thousand volunteers from 880 clinics swept through the country to deliver polio vaccine to 98 percent of four million children under five years old.

Supported by community leaders in every village, town and city in the country, trained volunteers went out to identify all the children under five. Using ice-boxes and cold packs when refrigeration was broken down, their forecasting ensured the vaccine doses were delivered in the right quantities at the right locations. Seven thousand teams, each with one vaccinator and one registrar fanned out to do the job in five miraculous days. UNICEF found ways to provide 10 million doses of polio vaccine in spite of difficulties with the UN Sanctions Committee.

Announcements were emblazoned on banners strung out across the busiest streets. The call to vaccinate went out from mosques, community organizations, schools and women's groups. Television spots ran every half hour reminding parents to vaccinate their children.

Goodness Outstrips Evil—But Is Under-Reported

Thus, the kaleidoscope of the future contains the two kinds of scenes juxtaposed on each other. Because the media does not report the non-zero-sum (win-win) events with anywhere near the frequency of the zero-sum (win-lose) events, we come to the conclusion that win-lose is all there is. In fact, goodness in human activity and consciousness likely outstrips evil in a ratio close to 99 to 1. Indeed, research on events printed in newspapers and broadcast on radio and TV indicates that ordinary human affairs are not news. It is only the extraordinary, the exceptional that is considered newsworthy by the world's editors. For the most part, terror and atrocity make the headlines, while good news items are relegated to the end or add-on position to provide a bit of relief to the unmitigated horror of what preceded them.

Our salvation lies in knowing where this kind of censorship leads, of working everywhere to focus the light of transparency, of truth-telling in the face of evil wherever it takes place, and focusing on the strengths, the virtues, the nobility of our common humanity, to turn the tide of anger towards the constructive use of human power and intent for the common good.

The generations of adults now in leadership positions in Western countries like Canada, the US, Britain, Australia, etc. need to step forward, to create goodness by example and to act with courage in the face of those who would harm our species and destroy our children's future and their legacy for their own greed and self-interest.

In our generation *doing no harm* will not be good enough to overcome the greatest challenge history ever delivered to any cohort of humanity. We need to act for good, knowing that in the international web of human communities in which we now live, each person's future is our future, and the future of all children is also our children's legacy.

What We Must Do

Those millions of us searching for higher ground, pushing to embrace human consciousness, seeking the wisdom of the sacred purpose and meaning of our species presence on the Earth at this time need to find ways to connect, so that our acting together becomes known, becomes exceptional and is seen as news.

And we need to withdraw our affirmation for past and present actions that may have led to victory but at the terrible expense of the victims.

And we need to so loudly applaud the courage and heroism of both ordinary citizens and leaders who do good, that we drown out in volume the tirades being vented for the purpose of fanning fear, hatred and anger.

Most of all, we need to *condemn messages from every source*—from media, from text books, from the pulpit—that encourage the young towards anger and rage, towards win-lose actions, towards self-destruction as suicide bombers. We need to speak out and shine a glaring light on those who deliberately strive to fill human consciousness with a force for evil. If we do this, we will do more to create a legacy of peace in our grandchildren's generation than any team of investigators searching for chemicals, biological agents or nuclear weapons of mass destruction.

The answer to the innocent childlike question, "Why do they hate us?" is clear. They hate us as a learned response to the teaching of those who would use their culture or their God's purpose as a mask or subterfuge for their real agenda of asserting their own power at the expense of others.

Deep in the core ethos, in the wisdom of all the world's sacred sources, from ancient times to the present, is the opposite message; the message that God's and humanity's central purpose is *love*; the message that we have been created in such a way as to protect and nurture the generations that follow, allowing them to grow towards greater complexity and greater goodness. This is the evidence of history.

Whether for secular motive or religious conviction we need to *unmask the distortion of truth.* If from the tens of thousands of human communities in which we live we connect, we join forces to speak this simple truth, the power of our common voice will be enormous.

To this strategic task for good I personally intend to bend every effort, and I invite you to do the same.

June, 2003

What Then Can We Do?

A Response to Acts Against Humanity

Desmond has recently returned from a trip to Japan, and had described a visit to Nagasaki where he was enormously touched by their memorial to those who died and were affected by the terrible day the bomb was dropped. As I listened, I was immediately transported in my mind out of time and space to the Holocaust Museum in Jerusalem, which I had visited in the spring of 1994. I remembered vividly my own experience of intense grief at the sights and scenes of unspeakable atrocity inflicted by the other side in this World War II conflict on the opposite side of the world in Europe. Who could forget the sight of the baby's shoe left in haste as a family fled; the fear-filled eyes of tormented people; and especially the hollow intoning of names of the innocent children counted in millions who were the victims of a conflict they did not create.

Forgiveness Is Not Enough

Whatever rationalization we give to live with such heart-wrenching horror, what remains for me is the certainty that there truly is evil in the world. It starts in unforgiving chain reaction from those who begin it, to those who for their own greedy or fearful benefit collude along the way. While it behooves us personally to let go, to forgive, to do what the people of Nagasaki are doing – this is just not enough! The responsibility for these atrocities remains on the conscience and in the deep soul future of every perpetrator. The issue for those of us who can see this wickedness for what it is, is how to ensure such villains do not get another chance in our lifetime or in the future to act at all, let alone with the impunity our century has extended to many of them.

What To Do

To understand what to do we must look to the other side of the equation—to those millions of ordinary folk who acted with courage, indeed, who often gave their lives to stop the insanity, and to those who acted in the face of great personal danger to take the roles of those whom the Israelis call "righteous gentiles." We find them on both sides of the warring parties. They saved whom they could and nurtured the wounded and afflicted. Some of these righteous ones, and many whom they saved, still live among us to model what must be done.

In response to each unspeakable act of evil we must raise ten million flags for good. No matter what benefit is promised, in democratic countries we must never vote for those whose policy or agenda is built on harming others. Especially in our ordinary everyday lives we must stand up and fight for decent action whether the wrong is perpetrated against us or anyone else. It is not good enough to say, "It doesn't involve us... Let them work it out... I'm okay... I'll just walk away from this." To act like this in small ways allows whole generations to adopt values which could lead to their collusion in some future time with those who would perpetrate crimes against individuals, nations and races.

The central value that could and would make a quality future possible is the understanding of our connectedness beyond nation, and the centrality of the planet and its life and living systems. This we all share. Their well-being ultimately will determine a quality future for each of us.

In the same way as time is a human invention that nature does not need or respect, so national borders are an idea of the same category. The air, the plants, the birds do not attend to national boundaries.

As we understand at deep human levels that behaviour and values in our own country spill over our borders and indeed across our planetary home, we will develop a code of action which if applied with respect and honour to our neighbours and our local environment will also affect our international outcomes.

We will learn to integrate ourselves as global citizens with a planetary worldview of the future. We will pay attention to the words and deeds of planetary elders like Robert Muller, former Assistant Secretary General of the UN and Chancellor Emeritus of the UN University for Peace in Costa Rica. We will become mentors and models to the generations that follow us, and especially to the youngest generations who will inherit our legacy and values. We do not have the luxury of saying it is up to the next generation to save the world. Instead, we must act to look after the world as a family looks after its home.

Hillary Clinton's notion that it takes a village to raise a child is a key issue here. If we are to preserve the Earth and allow for a future for our descendants different from what we have known in this last century of brutal wars and destruction, we must make the choice now to act with courage, to lead with higher values on respect for human dignity and planetary stewardship, to model and mentor right action at every opportunity. In this way we will raise the millions of flags for good every day. We must each of us be vigilant within our personal and community space that no act that promotes harm goes unchallenged. What we truly believe must not only be done; *we must be seen to be doing it and choosing to do it in partnerships, together and with others.*

I remain in all this the optimist that we are up to the tasks of courage required. This month as the Midwest of the North American continent fought the worst floods of the century, millions of people demonstrated how to work together in the face of great adversity.

Let there be a testament to "Never Again" for Nagasaki, for the Holocaust, and for all the victims of the crimes against our humanity, and against our planetary home.

May, 1997

Personal Stories:

Further Journeys of Second Adulthood

Thus I emerge from my pilgrimage to visit the sites of antiquity with renewed faith that the "new Jerusalem of the heart" can truly be built, not over the ashes and ruins of our common traditions, but by honouring them all, by respect for what they said and meant about the most divine idea of all—that we live together as one family, among a family of nations, in awe of our common humanity and the divinity in us and around us.

Moving to Higher Ground:

How Do We Do This?

The subtitle of this article is an open question. A variety of answers will emerge in this newsletter and in the first months of the journey of the Institute of Ethical Leadership. Of course, the specifics will be subjective and individual. At the same time, principles and considerations will be common. I will begin with these.

To answer, I spent the week-end of February 7-8, 1998 awaiting the birth of my new grandson and the call to grandparent duty for my 21 month-old granddaughter in enforced idleness and intense contemplation of the above question.

Intuitively, I kept returning to the place and time where as high school graduate I had to decide what to do next. Secretarial possibilities and the One-Year Teacher option were the common choices of the women of my generation. They were the fast track to material comforts, marriage and early family. In the interim one could expect the rewards of adolescent girlhood: fancy clothes, holidays, good times, etc.

A few of my good friends and I chose another option, to go to University for what we considered an indefinite forever, 5-10 years at least, to remain dependent minors, to work during holiday time to afford the next year's fees, etc. You know the story.

And what do I remember as my rewards? First, I remember the time as golden days and nights. I saw myself in libraries late at night, preparing term papers, studying for interminable exams, and... The next images come fast tumbling over one another I remember getting off the bus on Sherbrooke Street on a snowy Montreal morning at the Roddick Gates of McGill, and walking up the avenue of old, old trees overarching the roadway, the snow laden branches creating a winter fairyland, amid hundreds of my class mates, a movement of young men and women.

I remember greeting others and being greeted as we headed towards the Arts Building and an English lecture in Moyse Hall. I remember lunch times in the local greasy spoons and Student Union, arguing politics, or for or against an argument presented by the professor that morning; and late dinners at Le Caveau, the little French-Italian bistro just below Sherbrooke Street where you could stay for three hours over a bowl of cheap food and glass of wine.

I remember riding the trains with my debating team mates all over Quebec and New England, practicing the fine points of our arguments, joking and laughing. I remember walking up Mount Royal at Carnival Time among singing friends, with torch held high, to arrive at the skating rink, and the dance floor at the summit, amid sounds of jitterbug music and the smell of hot chocolate. And I remember summers, doubling over with laughter as we pushed our friend's Mini Minor up the very same road to attend the Mountain Playhouse, and afterwards ride down in comfort.

In other words, I remember life juicy and real with others, who also made the long commitment to become, to reach for what we thought in those days was higher ground.

Two factors emerge in my recollection. First, the commitment to hang in there for the long haul, regardless of the battles and the opportunities along the way. To get up day after day and just *do it*. Second, the bonding with others, each with their own struggles, their own agenda, to be there to graduate. Most of those who did went on to achieve successful lives and careers. It seemed so much simpler and easier in those days, in recollection of course, because there were many moments for us requiring courage and determination. Out of this comes the essence of what is needed to collaborate in the creation of the Institute for Ethical Leadership.

Over a lifetime, all of us can remember special moments in a seminar or learning situation, listening to a speech or attending an event. Then the moment passes, the event and people retreat into the past as our focus moves to deal with the challenges of the present. Eventually, nothing or very little remains. To change this outcome we need to provide something different. I would like to call it *sustained* initiative, where we form the kind of commitment we did as younger folk to school, a job, a career, a community enterprise, with the determination to build, to develop personally and collectively. Because that's how I believe we do a "juicy" meaningful life; and importantly, that's how we achieve a goal of a life and community based on decent ethical principles.

The rewards on the way may not be the more common one chosen by others, like position and recognition, material wealth and what it can buy, but it will be the kind of experience I remembered as a young woman: times of fun, joy and profound hopefulness that we together and individually can make a difference, can leave a legacy to our children and grandchildren that is more than just wealth.

In the end, it will be not what we talked about, but what we did, how we acted, where we put our time and energy, because by everything we do we model and mentor what we value. Our lives speak loudly to the future.

It is therefore with great enthusiasm that I put my hand, heart and mind to this initiative, to stay the course. I look forward to the journey and to the opportunity to walk again with new friends from the Roddick Gates to the Arts Building and up the mountain road to the summit at Mount Royal.

February, 1998

The Joy of Flow

Almost everyone can remember a special moment in life when time stood still, space was expansive, bodily sensation retreated into the background to make room for a heart-pulsing experience. So intense and directed is such a moment that it allows escape from the ordinary boundaries of skin to some kind of transcendence. This "flow" experience, both intensely real and paradoxically mystical, etches itself forever on the pathways of mind. We are transformed.

Two questions arise. Why does this happen, and how can we learn from such experiences to create the potential for more of them? I say "create the potential" because we can never force these experiences. They happen spontaneously when all the conditions are right. We help make the conditions right by cultivating a ready heart and mind. In this way the world's geniuses have composed great music, written enduring works of literature, and produced breakthrough scientific invention. But what about the rest of us? Let us return to the two questions of why do they happen and how can we learn to increase their frequency.

It is important to understand that these experiences occur at the margins of our abilities and talents; at the challenge level of what we have done before. For most of the time, the routines and patterns of our daily lives lock us into yesterday's limitations. But beyond this mundane and ordinary existence we can live our lives led by future visions of the possible. Here we embrace some larger *tomorrow-being* that we first discover in our minds. We are freed from current restrictions and can create a larger than life evolved self. In such playgrounds we are most likely to bump into other like-minded fellows. The opportunity arises to join forces with new friends and comrades for a purpose greater than any in yesterday's world.

Here in this exalted place of future vision we can dream of a better world for oneself and others. Here it is natural to focus on service since the needs of the yesterday-ego are forgotten in the excitement and adventure of future possibility. Those who experience these moments are forever changed. They continuously seek to recreate the feelings of exquisite joy this state of flow engenders. They push to work more and more at the upper margins of their abilities.

So, to create the potential for moments of flow experience, we must avoid focusing too narrowly on the past. If we do, we are trapped within the confines of our old selves and our old pasts. Unfortunately our institutions tend to enshrine such past behaviour in us. We are supported when we follow the expected routines. We are often challenged when we question or try to move beyond them. This is the reason that invention so frequently occurs outside the established venues. Here, free of the enormous burden of routine and past practice that consume life energy, the few acting in flow create new solutions in the rarefied air outside the walls. In such space they stand on the shoulders both of those who have gone before and their own life experience, and look to new horizons. If we wish to live in the experience of flow, we must join such adventurers and seekers of new tomorrows.

But be prepared. Such journeys demand both effort and courage. However, once intoxicated by the experience of flow, such adventurers are forever addicted, and what a life that makes! Forget retirement, forget aging. The human psyche so engaged has discovered that *youth is a state of mind and the future fueled by such thinking is the very power source of life.*

December, 1994

Pursuit of Personal Destiny:

The Israeli Connection

As the aircraft lifts off the tarmac out of London's Heathrow Airport on the second leg of our return journey to Vancouver from Tel Aviv, snippets of images of the last ten days in Israel float like a lighted collage across my mind's eye. Shabbat Dinner with Edna, our hostess, and her family; the day of gracious hospitality hosted by one of our students in her Arab village home; wonderful tastes of Israeli food; wine and sweet, strong Turkish coffee; and especially images of our students working with eager intensity and enthusiasm as we tried together to overcome the barriers of culture and language, only to find time and time again that the traditional wisdom of Judaism's prophets and sages supported the teaching principles we work with. Added to this was the surprising emergent memory of my childhood Hebrew language, assisted by the continuous instant translation of the more than willing participants, all of which made communication surprisingly easy.

Desmond and I watched with pride as our enthusiastic first class of Israeli Facilitators demonstrated their mastery of the skills and principles of Creative Learning, taught in English, but performed in Hebrew, while I struggled to translate for Desmond from a language I couldn't understand five days earlier.

It is interesting how the human qualities of enthusiasm, courage to act, gracious hospitality, warmth and generosity transcend both language and culture. Indeed, under the superficial patterns and routines of the lives of all of us, our intuition allows immersion in and connection to the universal current of life, where the histories of all people are connected. We see this especially in the smiling faces of the young people entering adulthood, who sit together to learn or share a meal.

Here, in this ancient land, modern Israel exists as a paradox of hope against a backdrop of danger. Here, more than anywhere, on a lighted centre stage for all the world to see, our deep common heritage, history and profound connectedness must overcome our superficial separateness. To play a tiny part in tipping the scales toward peace would be a sacred privilege for Desmond and me.

Pursuit of Personal Destiny

At deep intuitive levels we become immersed in the soul of the world. In this sacred space, a sure and certain knowing emerges that we are here in this time and place to pursue a mission of personal destiny. All the gifts, talents, experiences of our life are a prelude to this task. Yet many of us avoid experiencing life at this depth. We mislead ourselves to pursue more worldly goals without the real understanding that such accomplishments are but the platform for the real and true purpose of our lives.

Whenever we get even momentary glimpses that we are on the right track and that our action is in the direction of true purpose, waves of joy infuse us at this deep soul level, and provide energy and momentum to continue, no matter how hard the task, or what barriers are placed in front of us.

In Israel this past week, as Desmond and I watched our first group of Facilitators of Creative Learning demonstrate their newly won skills, a wave of that special joy washed over us.

How did we get to do this? It began in several places, over many years, but all were directed at bringing us to this past week.

In 1958 I represented my country at a gathering of Jewish youth from Israel and around the world at the University of Jerusalem. This first Jewish Youth Congress was convened by the then Prime Minister of Israel, David Ben Gurion. The image of this short, powerful man with a corona of white hair entering the hushed room with the flags of a hundred nations flying, and all of us standing to sing "Hatikva" (The Hope), the National Anthem, has been buried in my mind for almost forty years. It resurfaced when I searched my library for the yellowing book prepared to record the speeches of the event. My 19 year old self spoke innocently of creating cultural bridges between Israel and its brethren in the Diaspora.

In February, 1997 we had the not so innocent opportunity to begin the construction of this bridge with intention, using the tools of creative learning, the product of the last decade of our work. They grafted easily into place as time and time again they were affirmed by the wisdom of the Jewish sages quoted to us by our participants as we made some point or other.

And Desmond's book, *The Visioneers*, whose main action takes place in Israel, was the vehicle that opened the doors and minds of our Israeli hosts to invite us to come. Elsewhere in this Newsletter, in the "Address to the Graduates," Desmond speaks eloquently to our real Israeli Visioneers of the ideas and story conceived in his imagination more than half a decade ago. Thus the vision in the book and that of our Israeli hosts meld to create a new, very real outcome which allows the whole team of us to pursue our personal destinies.

The visioneering work we all came to do is urgently needed by this world, plunging as it is at breakneck speed into the 21st Century. Full of the energy of our own journey, we encourage you to consider your own mission and destiny, and pursue it for the sake of the soul of the world.

March, 1997

Written following working visits to Israel and Greece

What May We Build on the Ruins of Antiquity?

I write on Mother's Day, which for me is a symbolic honouring for the mothers of all time—the women who in their time on Earth birthed, nurtured and tutored each generation of our ancestors. While the contribution of fatherhood remains through built cities, temples, technology and the written thought and literature of our heritage, the contribution of motherhood is in the consciousness, the conscience and the spirit of our humanity.

Up to the present time the work and words of the more brutal part of our nature has predominated. However, in the generations now alive a new sensitivity is emerging to embrace the nobility and the divine in men and women. While at the start of the millennium its voices are weaker than the powerful expressions of competitive and rational thought, their number is growing, and in our time of rapid worldwide communication it will not take millennia until its message is clearly heard.

Visiting Ancient Places

I, too, walked through the same antiquities as Desmond. He and I saw something different. I marveled at the extraordinary architectural beauty of the temples and the statuary in ancient

Greece and the colourful spontaneity of the wall paintings of ancient Akrotiri. I was awestruck by the beauty and complexity of 7th century BCE Thera built by the Spartans with theatres, temples, stoas and residential houses, now spread about in ragged ruins atop one of the highest points on the island of Santorini.

I, too, looked over to the Temple Mount in Jerusalem to see the Golden Mosque of Islam built in the exact place where the magnificent Hebrew Temple stood before it. I know, too, of the great historical conquests of the Persians, the Greeks and the Romans, the Turks and so on. I was appalled at how the ruins I was looking at were the remains of civilizations destroyed not so much by time and natural disaster but by human intent.

The glorious Parthenon serves as a tragic example of such wanton destructiveness. A wonder of the ancient world, it survived almost intact for 2200 years—a tribute to various conquering nations who had preserved it over time. However, in the end, the conquering Turks degraded it to a munitions storage facility and it was blown apart 300 years ago when a Venetian cannon ball fired into it ignited the explosives. This intentional disregard for the accomplishments of preceding civilizations has been a repetitive story throughout history. Like the stories we tell ourselves about ourselves, we have made these acts the stories of heroes and winners without stopping to consider, to factor in, the terrible destruction and the suffering caused by these "heroic" hands to mothers and their children, and to whole civilizations of men and women who were simply going about the business of their daily lives.

I saw the temples as they fell and the people crouched in fear, or lying dead, or dispersed into the countryside, devastated like the live images we have seen on our television screens of the refugees of Europe and Africa. I saw the faces of Alexander the Great and the Roman conquerors meld and merge into the faces of Hitler, Saddam Hussein and the revolutionary thugs in Africa, and I cried for the mothers and fathers in antiquity who suffered the same fate of our current unfortunates, but who lie buried in the obscurity of history.

And yet, amidst all this, were those whose ideas called for peace. From the ancient pagan myths, the Logos, the Word, the divine Idea of the noblest of human thought came the values written down by the wise ones of antiquity—the ideas of living in peace, of loyalty, of compassion, of service to others.

These ancient moral codes enjoined us not to kill, or steal, or lie, or covet and were embraced 2000 years ago by the gentle teachings of the man from Galillee, who saw the suffering and spoke about the power of love, even towards the enemy.

Now in our time, two millennia on, does it not behoove us to look with new eyes—with compassion towards the suffering of our ancestors and with awe at what they built, but also with new judgment at their deeds of valour—to question what was "heroic" enough to earn the title of "the Great," and to redefine for our own time, and for the new millennium, what greatness and heroism really are.

A new vision of what was great about our past needs to emerge in the story of our survival as a species through war, through disaster, through plague and famine. We can see what happens in such devastation today. We watch with awe the international careworkers, the peacekeepers and the ordinary citizens from all over the world, who give and serve, and we can clearly see that just such unsung heroes of antiquity made it possible for us to survive. It was they, and not the Caesars and Alexanders, who were truly Great!

Which brings me to the wonderful experience of celebrating Passover in Israel, and to its meaning in relation to all of the above

Celebrating Passover in Israel

The Passover story related in the *Haggada* each Passover by Jews everywhere in the world ends in the Diaspora (countries outside Israel) with the forever ancient prayer "Next Year in Jerusalem." In our time when Jerusalem is accessible and welcoming to the international traveler, this has a different meaning. In my case, although I have been to Israel five times in my lifetime since I was 19, I had never spent Passover in Jerusalem. This year I achieved what was, for me, the prayer experienced.

This year in the midst of loving friends and their family not far from Netanya, about 50 miles north west of Jerusalem, I found myself hearing the same story and singing the same songs that were part of my childhood experience in Montreal so long ago. What an extraordinary privilege to hear all this in their language of origin and to eat the food prepared by many family friends. I could not help but imagine this same scene across the millennia in millions of places. Here it was the Passover, as in ancient Thera it was some feast to celebrate another story or set of beliefs.

Here was humanity in the family, celebrating with food and wine, song and laughter and story. Here was the juice, the passion, the emotion, the spirit for which all these temples were built in the first place. And here, too, was the good life of the future for millennia to come. Here were the very qualities that allowed our survival—love of children, love of each other, commitment to service, camaraderie and belief in the future. "Next year in Jerusalem!"

The New Jerusalem

Thus I emerge from my pilgrimage to visit the sites of antiquity with renewed faith that the "new Jerusalem of the heart" can truly be built, not over the ashes and ruins of our common traditions, but by honouring them all, by respect for what they said and meant about the most divine idea of all—that we live together as one family, among a family of nations, in awe of our common humanity and the divinity in us and around us.

The story of Passover is the story of the winning of freedom over oppression. It is the story for which we have lived since it was first told. Its theme is universal. May we honour the heroes and the heroines then and now, who stood up for such victories. May we commit ourselves to vision a world where the human spirit for goodness spreads its light over our family of nations.

June, 2000

Questions of Meaning
and Lessons from
the Ancient Prophets

These past months of summer and early fall have been crowded with the kinds of events that jolt one's thinking out of the present into past and future. Some of the outward journeys have been reported in the previous pages. Others include the growth of two grandchildren still under a year old.

These two young ones raise the question of what life and the world will be like when they are grandparents. With that thought one's attention is drawn back to a seeming "simpler" time, when our grandparents were in the same place. Such questioning leads me to considering the central myth of our time. Intuitively, I reject the notion that we are "accidental beings in an accidental universe." I begin to search for a more meaningful description of who we are.

New information in both cosmology and studies of antiquity challenge our current knowledge of the universe and our planet. Stars have been found that seem to be older than we thought the universe to be. Was something there before the beginning? New planets have been found orbiting distant stars. All this challenges known cosmological data and cries out for new thinking.

New dates for humanoid fossils found in Asia are confirmed to almost two million years. The foundations of the Sphinx appear to have known the weathering effect of flowing water from a time much earlier than experts had thought the monument dated. Remains of human sites are found in Calgary in Canada dated at 22,000 years, a full 10,000 years before other earliest known evidence of human community in North America. Cave paintings are found in Australia dating back an incredible 75,000 years. Deep history projects reveal ancient goddess-based culture much earlier than imagined.

My own belief is that the trickle of evidence will soon become a flood and will force a complete change in worldview. In order for our images of who we are in time and place not to be swept away, we must begin to prepare a new metaphoric ark.

I have the sense that human beings now living on the Earth and continuing into a predictable short-term future, are occupying a tiny part of a living cosmos too vast for human imagination. We are inheritors of an antiquity so ancient that the beginning must retreat to a thought in the mind of God.

I am reminded here of a new story that Desmond has written. It is an allegory called "Antale," which tells the story of the world of the ants. Like us, they thought that they and what they could see was all there was. When they discovered that it wasn't, the important accompanying realization was that they had to care more carefully for their own world.

How then are we to attribute meaning to our time and place and work for the betterment of our world? I am drawn to ask again the questions with which I began. Who are we *really*? Where are we going in our future and the future of our children and grandchildren?

What emerges for me is a sense of extraordinary wonder and awe of the nobility lodged in our humanity and its consciousness, whose heritage is so ancient, and so marvelously renewed in the miracle of the birth of a newborn child. Even if these ideas are not yet understood as a specific myth or story, they lead to "knowing" that life is infused with divine meaning, which is continuously revealed as we open our minds to understand. If what we see in the tiny microcosm of our present view is such a marvel, *what might the real macrocosm be?*

As we adopt the view of awe and wonder, the work of service

ahead becomes clearer. We, the cohort of six billion now alive, must preserve the best of our heritage for the future, as a sacred trust of our generations to our descendants. This includes the stewardship of our planet and the nurturing of human cultural diversity so far developed.

Interestingly, lessons of how we might do this can come from the sacred books and stories of our ancestors, who also wondered about such questions.

In Genesis Chapter 18 in the Old Testament of the Hebrew and Christian Bible, Abraham argues with God to save the city of Sodom, where his nephew, Lot, lives. Abraham starts with the suggestion that God save the city if fifty "good men" can be found living there. He bargains it down to ten, but Sodom is so wicked that not even that small number can be found. So God saves Lot, but destroys the city.

What this suggests is that in ancient times, as well as today, societies were from time to time in grave danger of collapse from causes created by themselves. In Biblical times, God sent prophet after prophet to warn the people to seek repentance and a change of ways and heart. In one such story (Jonah, Chapter 3) God sent Jonah to warn the people of Nineveh about their wickedness. In this case, the king, as an authority figure, paid attention and convinced the people to change, and so the city was saved.

In our time we are very much in need of leaders and the metaphorical ten "good men" (and women) in every community, and in the global village as a whole. Using networks to spread news and ideas, models for good can act to impact the whole world, thus magnifying the work of the original ten by connecting them to like-minded others wherever they live and work.

When I consider the possibility for *good*, I am awestruck and hopeful to think of the future that *can be* for my own children and grandchildren, and for yours.

October, 1996

Notes from the Journey of Second Adulthood:

A Stop at Avebury

A few kilometers into my journey of second adulthood, on a sunny morning in November, I hold a fragment of pottery in my hand collected this summer at Avebury, a sacred site in ancient Britain. My fragment shows natural symbols, parts of a bird in flight, plants and flowers. Focusing all my senses on this tiny particle of another time, I try to conjure up the culture and the people who made it. My trained intellect produces a list of deductions including use of natural symbols, quality of artistry, and the technology of the larger vessel of which it was a part.

To reach beyond my sensory viewpoint I close my eyes. Instantly a blue sky appears. The soft air fills with the sound of flying wings and the cry of birds. The sacred chalk-white stones of Avebury stand glistening on a sunlit hill. From every direction people gather, moving towards the sacred circle, tramping through tall wild grass and fields of wild flowers. Suddenly I am among them, carrying the water jug from which the fragment came that I had held before. We gather in peace to celebrate our humanity and our connection with nature and each other.

The scene, unique in colour and marked by the circle of stones of Avebury, is replaced by another and another, each different in detail and conversation, but the same in theme, rhythm and feeling. Each is surrounded by a larger energy field that I can feel rather than see. From this vantage point I reach beyond my sense-imprisoned reality, beyond the hill top of my own life's experience into a vast, timeless universe where wave after wave of previous civilizations emerge, grow, decline and disappear. Without warning thunder rolls in and lightning strikes the ground beside me. The jug I am carrying falls from my hand, smashing on the stones at my feet. I reach down to pick up a fragment. Reality floods my senses again and I see only the piece I hold in my hand.

A slight shift of mind and rhythm cannot, however, erase the sense of exhilaration that comes from seeing the vast network of human connection across time and space. The mind is overwhelmed by the profound sense of what life means—the elegance of its simplicity, the awesome complexity of its diversity. I understand that as I focus on the fragment with my senses and my intellect, it fills my conscious mind. But when I retreat from my intellect, the whole of my unconscious merges with an ever present noosphere, and my imagination conjures up the possibilities of what was here.

From this we understand that our conscious mind is only a fragment of the jug. As we hold on to it in fear and examine it with our senses, we see a tiny particle of the whole of which we are a part. We act mistakenly, as if the reality of our senses is all there is, even though we know how often they have misled us in the past to see ourselves separate from nature and from each other.

Wars, violence, assassins' bullets, and separatism of every kind result from the fear-filled consciousness of those who see only a fragment of reality. The role of those of us who have caught a glimpse of the bigger picture is to tell as many others as we can, and to act with the larger truth in mind. We can and should use our expanded consciousness to actively promote every form of human communication that exposes it. Eventually, there will be too much shared knowledge, the secret will be revealed, and the tight control over the present view of reality will be broken.

The above thoughts lead me now to comment on another way the new reality is revealed. Two new sources of information come into view. One is the film *Powder*, written and directed by Victor Salvo. The other is the new novel Desmond has just completed.

Powder tells the story of a boy whose mother was struck by lightning in an incident that precipitated his birth and her death. He was raised in secret by grandparents who had no way of understanding his strange power. They exposed his mind to books and shielded him from the world. He emerges with incredible genius and a consciousness evolved well past our late 20th century capacity to feel our connectedness with other living beings. With the exception of a few benefactors, Powder is treated with disdain by his contemporaries as he is exposed to the heart throbbing violence supposedly typical of male teenage culture. Responding with a mind evolved beyond fear and astounding mental and physical power, he turns aside the moment's terror with such a profound gentleness of spirit that he earns at least temporarily their grudging respect. In one memorable scene on a camping trip with his class an adult hunter wantonly shoots a deer. Powder forces the man to experience the anguish of the dying animal as if it were his own death. The hunter and the witnesses discover a new awareness of connectedness.

Desmond's latest novel, *Antale*, is an allegory about ants whose world and events model our own 20th century history and thinking. The exciting story line builds crisis upon crisis until the very future hangs in the balance, waiting for new choices. In one of the most powerful scenes, thousands of inhabitants of Antale crowd the courtyard of one of their great cities, waiting in breathless anticipation for the report from an explorer from beyond the "Rim," hoping for salvation. In graphic detail she tells of a world thousands of years post destruction still pouring poisons into dead air. Salvation must come from another source. Here, too, the author's sweeping imagination points to a new kind of evolving consciousness as the necessary condition to change the future in profound and unpredictable ways.

Both authors paint with brush strokes of stark reality the danger to life and our planet being brought by our present course of thinking. Both show that the reality we know is but a fragment of a whole. "Out there" are new possibilities that are really "in here." There is hope for our species if we can deliver a new mind and heart.

From all of this, two issues emerge for me. First, from their experience with their own transliminal ability to access their unconscious minds, millions of credible, ordinary people can now bear personal witness to the phenomenon that the conscious mind is not all there is. The outpouring of stories by every kind of media is pushing old paradigms out of the way. Just as cognitive science began to explore the effect of thought on behaviour as soon as it was clear that there was something in the forbidden black box, i.e., consciousness, so a newly emerging cohort of neuroscientists will use scientific tools, perhaps of a different kind, to investigate the holoverse and surrounding magnetic fields beyond conscious awareness. As in the amazing discoveries now coming in from the Hubble telescope in space showing cosmic marvels beyond imagination and anticipation, the new research in the neurosciences will produce a bonanza of information destined to push our quality of life beyond the known boundaries.

The second point is that the story tellers who create the lighted pathway to discovery are grounded in the solid knowledge of our time. Just as earlier myth makers took advantage of their noosphere, so the quasi science fiction of a *Powder*, or an *Antale*, or *The Visioneers* may be closer to the truth than we think.

So, knowing this, what do we do? In life each of us must choose a cause. I leave you to consider yours. For me, I choose in my second adulthood quest to discover the storytellers and the myth-breaking thinkers, then find the ways to combine my own voice with theirs to get the secret out.

November, 1995

Last Words

We can enter this "prime time of our lives" at any age, and we can stay vibrant and vigorous so long as we continue to engage the soul wisdom, sometimes called intuition, to know the right thing to do. Here is where human consciousness, which is ageless, makes us so different from the plants of my first metaphor.

The Vibrant Years*:

Soul Time in the Human Life Span

Our youth-oriented culture undervalues life as years pass. Nature images abound: we are a seed .. a bud... a flower... a wilted blossom... dry petals crumbling... dust to dust. We are compared to seasons: born in spring, flourish in summer at our prime, fade in autumn, die in winter. What an over-simplification! We are not plants, concerned only to survive and propagate the next generation. We are born. We grow. We grow and grow. Some of us decline at an early time; others continue to grow and learn and make a contribution to the next generation over a lifetime. Milton Erikson, who identified the stages of human life almost a half century ago, called the stage of life I am about to describe the age of "generavity," the time when concern moves from focus on personal gain to the larger issues of life, to see the long view, the fuller picture, to contribute to the growth of the next generation. It is this time of life I would like to call "the age of the soul." It is in these years that we enter soul time.

Unlike our physical maturity, we do not enter this time within a particular chronological age range, as one enters puberty or menopause. Nor is it certain everyone will reach this time. In fact, some young people live a good portion of their lives in soul time, while some very old people retreat from their prime to such self concern that their childish behaviour defeats even their most generous caregivers. We can enter this "prime time of our lives" at any age, and we can stay vibrant and vigorous so long as we continue to engage the soul wisdom, sometimes called intuition, to know the right thing to do. Here is where human consciousness, which is ageless, makes us so different from the plants of my first metaphor.

At any time of our life we can choose to act with the vigour of youth, tempered with the wisdom of soul to participate in right acting, sometimes in a leadership role, but also comfortable in followership. As we act in cooperation with others, in concert, in coherence, our mind and spirit engages the body's immune systems to pour the neurochemical messengers of strength, power and good health into the part of our body that is ageless, the inner spirit that is truly us. We are continuously renewed and refreshed with a vibrancy that lights our way and shines out to light the paths of others.

Welcome the Mensch and the Old Soul

Various names have been given to people of any age observed to be living in soul time. One of these is the Jewish concept of "a mensch," a decent person who sees human higher possibility in all people, who can be counted on to do the right thing, regardless of personal cost. A mensch is a person who sees the mensch in others, soul to soul. Another name is "old soul," a person who acts in a way that displays human nobility, sometimes even in the face of treachery. I have seen such behaviour in a five year old, concerned about "Mummy's feelings" when he was in personal danger. I have seen it in a young woman working selflessly to save our country, and in a seventy-two year old person willing to share his life to save the planet. The criterion is not the chronological age, but the maturity and the wisdom that underlies the person's value system.

But it is more than a value system. The age in which we live is too dangerous, and the matters at hand too urgent for the luxury of armchair philosophizing. Values need to be expressed in action. Such action must be outward looking, embracing the larger, longer perspective about the critical issues of our time—peace, the environment, and the new learning and thinking we will need if civilization is to flourish in a new century full of discontinuities.

Action in the face of urgency and danger takes courage. Here we come again to the issue of a person's age. It is not that years of living are required to act the mensch, but that many of us use our years of experience to become less fearful. We learn how to exercise our powerful minds and spirits more readily.

This phenomenon has a practical outcome for each of us. Unlike the plants of earlier reference that exist the same in millions of copies, we are unique. Our learning, our life experience and hard won successes mean that the contribution of each of us is a specialized piece or thread of an eternal tapestry. Woven together, the fabric creates a mighty and awesome picture. This has an important lesson for leaders. Wherever we can collaborate, cross fertilize, work as part of a team, we can maximize the effect of our effort. Working together creates "emergences" of higher order. All over the world we see the truth of this. The peace process in the Middle East and Northern Ireland inches forward as ancient enemies learn to work together. The environment benefits as groups on both sides of the issues cooperate. Businesses flourish as they harmonize their efforts to serve the needs of their clients.

Thus, to live vibrantly every day of our lives, to live in soul time, we need to engage the ageless wisdom of our highest and noblest selves, and we need to do this in the company of like-minded others. Such a cohort of leaders will evolve the consciousness of our species and create a legacy of hope for the next millennium.

February, 1996

From a book title by Francis MacNab.

Act to Change the World:

The Biological Basis of Acts of Courage

Is it possible at any point on life's journey to have an experience of new thinking so profound that it changes the rest of your life? The point of discontinuity between a personal past and personal future often happens in a flash to those who have had an urgent life crisis and have "seemingly died." In these suspended moments between life and life people give a surprisingly consistent and positive account of some kind of consciousness survival. The experience produces a sense of deep felt joy and exhilaration that spills over into the rest of their life. It appears to quiet for their future the fear of death and they gain access to a "living afterlife" which is both joyous and heroic.

Can those of us who have not suffered from such trauma learn vicariously from others' experiences about how to live the rest of our lives? Could we create with intention a moment of profound transformative thought based on some new understanding of the true nature of consciousness? Looking from the platform of present state scientific knowledge about what must be happening in "near death experiences," we might learn what makes them so consistent across the human species, in spite of enormous culture-laden differences in their meaning.

To answer this question we must begin from a different place in our understanding of our universe that what most people still believe. In the following quote from *The Reflexive Universe* Arthur

Middleton Young (1905-1995) makes the case eloquently when he says, "The older concept of a universe made up of physical particles interacting according to fixed laws is no longer tenable. It is implicit in present findings that *action* rather than matter is basic."

"*Action* rather than matter is basic." This is the clue we need. The cycles of birth, life, death and rebirth are experienced as dynamic *waves of action*. This teeming, flowing life force includes consciousness, especially human consciousness. It has a biological basis anchored in action. This means that as we act positively to enhance life, to serve it, we *catch the life wave* and release into our system the ingredients of well-being and exhilaration. Much scientific research demonstrates that the positive indicators of healing and well-being are enhanced by doing good work, by feeling good about the work you do, and even by observing others doing good work (the Mother Teresa Effect).

In their near death experiences, people catch the life wave so powerfully that they are released from the ultimate fear, the fear of not surviving. They see that they are going to this wonderful place where consciousness survives. They *know* they will survive, and it is marvelous. The path for the rest of life, therefore, is cleared for fearless acts of bravery, service and courage in a much more tranquil inner environment. The biological consequences of such thinking permeate the psyche and fill the whole being with new power. The person becomes a new man or new woman.

Some people, having been convinced in a less physically traumatic way of these concepts that also produce a tranquil interior environment and acts in their lives to continuously create the feeling of exhilaration and "love of life" that infuses all of their actions. It gives them an authenticity that is unmistakable and very inspiring to others.

My friend, Robert Muller, is such a person. I do not wish to embarrass him here by so acknowledging his special quality, but it is important for the world to know. Robert's philosophy is reflected in everything he writes, but especially in his poem *Decide to be Happy*. Here he encourages us "to live passionately your miraculous life" and "to feel God in your body, mind, heart, and soul and be convinced of eternal life and resurrection." Anyone who knows 72 year old Robert, who has just fallen in love and is soon to be married, is aware of the incredible energy emanating from some deep source of his being. This exhilaration has the same biological basis as the near death experience that suspends fear and makes possible a continuous flow of good and courageous acts of service to humanity.

But what about the rest of us mortals who neither have had a physical near death experience nor are endowed with the psychological power of a Robert Muller? Can we, too, create a suspended moment between life and life? I believe we can. A poem I wrote titled "Yes" describes this possibility.

Yes is an affirmation built on a thousand noes... Yes begins with intention to take little yes steps... so that when the chorus of yeses rings out in celebration, fuelling the heart with wild courage (the biological basis of exhilaration) it is easy to take giant leaps...*

Thus the formula for life after life may be written by the reader of this essay in a set of personal acts of courage—a personal "Yes" poem. Your chorus of yeses will be in keeping with your own special and unique contribution to serve humankind. It could be your personal blueprint for transformation.

In Conclusion

I have become convinced over a life time of acting in the world that there is a seemingly magical force in the very act of acting that creates the energy enough to achieve the dream. This force is not accessible to the timid, but once harnessed, it can and does change the world. It is the fuel that releases the life force itself.

So, the idea is to choose to act. Choose to act in your own way, in synchrony with *your* dreams, using your talent to serve in your community, however you define that word. Be out and about in the world, thinking about how you can best better the human condition and with it the planet and all of the rest of its creatures. You will catch the wave. Your personal reward will be an internal, biologically based sense of well-being so profound you will change not only your own future, but also all those exposed to your shining model. You will live in your own life after life.

July, 1995

—————————————
*Yes (1), page xxiii. Yes (2), page xxvii.

125

Afterword

The layered stories of personal journeys become the fabric and texture of every novel, every poem, every biography ever written, whether admitted or not. Cloaked and disguised in an infinite variety of forms, they allow the reader to see only the shadow of these intense moments of insight and clarity that comes when such thoughts are written down as they are experienced, channeled as it were from some deep internal space. The poems included in the Prologue, hidden from view until now, are offered as a gift of my personal truth.

The essays that follow are a more explicit example of a similar phenomenon. The journey I have described is very common and readers may certainly recognize part of their own life's adventures and misadventures in the poetry and stories that connect them. Most importantly this book is meant to describe the hope that each of us harbours intensely, ... *to love and be loved in return at whatever age or stage of life we are now in and to make a worthy and meaningful contribution so that in the end, our lives have made a difference.*

It is a great privilege to live such a life and I am continuously filled with the wonder of tomorrow's possibility.

Acknowledgments

The essays in this collection were written based on wide reading of books, journals, newspapers, magazines, etc. Wherever the ideas are directly taken from particular sources this is noted in the interior of the text and wherever whole books or journal articles directly influenced thinking they are noted in the Endnotes referenced by essay title, so the reader can see and follow through on these sources if they are interested in doing so.

Since these essays were written for an international, national and local community of friends and colleagues who subscribed to "The Visioneer Newsletter," they are truly written as deeply felt communication, conversation as it were, on topics of serious and mutual interest.

Since this is not an academic text, the reference and sources are not as rigorously set out as they would be in that kind of written work. At the same time I am an academic and have had a clear intention to give credit to appropriate sources. Of course wide reading influences thought and perspective in unique ways and I may have missed recognizing the particular source of some ideas. I thank all these sources for helping to shape my mind and thought with their work.

On the other hand these essays are somewhat like the poems. The thoughts grew and shifted until I was ready to write. They always emerged whole at one sitting like the poems, and like them they were passionately felt. I do not apologize for this passion, the exuberance or even the flag waving. As a woman, a mother and person who has experienced deeply, the 20th century with its wars, violence, injustice, anti-Semitism, as well as its noble advances in all kinds of thinking, in human rights, in technology and especially in ecumenism, I feel I have earned the right and have the responsibility to speak my mind and express my personal authentic heartfelt truths. These essays should therefore be read with that in mind.

It is my fervent hope and dream that readers will see a legitimate and valuable perspective of such a woman's journey and allow their reading to influence their own journeys in positive and appropriate ways.

Endnotes

Part II: Relationships

Relationships, Partnerships and Alliances: The Energy Source That Can Save the Planet

29   Editorial, "A look back at the best of the year 2003", *Vancouver Sun*, Friday January 2, 2004

33   "Women on Top", *Shared Vision*, January 2004.

33   Founded in 1980 as a source of investment and support for social entrepreneurs, Ashoka is a global organization that elects Ashoka Fellows in more than 48 countries. For more information about the Ashoka Foundation visit www.ashoka.org

Part III: Wisdom

The Evolution of Consciousness: Scientific Evidence for Win-Win as the Basic Principle Underlying Life

60   Seligman, Martin E.P., *Authentic Happiness*, Free Press, 2002

61   Wright R, *Non-Zero: The Logic of Human Destiny*, Pantheon, 2000

62   Lazlo, Ervin, Macroshift, Bennett-Koehler, 2001.

Part VI: Anti Semitism

"Why Do They Hate Us?"

90   Martin Seligman, *Authentic Happiness*, New York: Free Press, 2002

90   Robert Wright, *Non-Zero: The Logic of Human Destiny*, New York: Pantheon, 2000.

91   Pierre Birnbaum, *The Anti-Semitic Moment: A Tour of France 1898*, Douglas and McIntyre, 2003.

92   "UN, Iraq and Polio" and "How Will the Arab World React?" *Timeline*, a bimonthly publication of the Foundation for Global Community, Issue 69, May/June 2003.

What Then Can We Do? A Response to Acts Against Humanity

98   Gillies, Douglas, *Prophet: The Hatmaker's Son: The Life of Robert Muller*, East Beach Press, 2002